BYE BYE BLACK SHEEP

CELESTE YVONNE WELLS

For information, permissions, or to request interviews, contact:

Printed in the United States of America
First Edition

ISBN: 979-8-218-57914-2

Cover design by : Euvizion Express, Eugene Davis

Bye Bye Black Sheep
Celeste Yvonne Wells

PROLOGUE

Fair warning; this book wasn't written to entertain you. Although at times it's entertaining and has enough ups, downs and plot twists for a major motion picture. The intention is not to glorify how easy it is to take advantage of the impressionable, the weak minded, and the needy. It is not designed to taunt those who are and have become prey to predators. It is not a nightmarish fairy-tale about a poor girl who hustled her way to the top, through crime and debauchery. My story is about never letting your circumstances determine who you are. Survival in its rawest form while still staying true to who I was. A story of a life born from choices I made, and lessons learned the hard way.

I once called myself the Master of manipulation and crime.

Even though my reign is over, my legend lives on through the memories of those who've traveled this road with me, and through the actions of those who have followed in my footsteps. My actions have affected many people, and they will continue to, for as long as people know my name.

Although I am not proud of many of the things I've done, I have a story that is worth telling—a story that's rooted in what's left of the streets today. The streets are a stage and everybody is playing a part, where betrayal and derailment are dressed up in gold chains, and a place where survival is often confused with success.

I was born **Celeste Yvonne Wells** on March 21, 1956, to Iris and Chester Wells, Jr., in Miami Beach, Florida, at Mt. Sinai Hospital. From birth, it seemed that my fate was written. But still, no parent ever knows what the future holds for their child. Our humble beginnings may have signified that a struggle was underway for me, but my parents could not have imagined the eventual life of deception and trouble that I would live.

This isn't just about what I did, but why. It's about the environment I came from, the people I looked up to, and the survival mindset that shaped my early years. I was caught in a cycle that pulled in women like me who had nothing to lose—where quick money seemed like the only option, and where the risks I took felt normal.

But time has a way of offering clarity. And eventually, the same streets that once gave me a sense of control became the ones I had to leave behind to save my life.

Today, life is a different place for me—where I feel no shame in telling my story because of how I've seen it serve as a survival guide to others. Oftentimes your testimony can be the difference in being written off or given a second chance.

This is my second chance.

CONTENTS

CHAPTER 1

Miami Herald; November 26, 1989.

Metro Police have arrested a 33-year-old woman they say is the leader of "the fingernail bandits," a group of well-dressed women who sport long fingernails and are suspected of at least 30 thefts. Celeste Yvonne Wells was arrested by detective Dehlia Bailey at the Metro Justice Building on Monday when she appeared at a hearing to face burglary and weapons charges. Wells was charged with five counts of forgery, three counts of grand theft, and one count of petty theft. Monday's arrest was Wells's 61st, Bailey said. Wells also has 31 separate aliases and a 10-page FBI rap sheet. Wells allegedly led a group of five or six women who preyed on salesclerks in stores and travel agencies throughout Dade County. The women, who range in age from 16 to 30, were distinguished by their nice clothes, fake Caribbean accents, and three-to-four-inch fingernails. Their methods were simple but effective.

1989 was a salty-sweet year for me. At the time this article was published I was slowly coming down off of a nearly 20-year run of crime. Everything about this particular newspaper clipping summed up who I had been up until that point. Still to this day, it's like an obituary for a version of myself that no longer exists. A version of me who not only went by different names but who had different interests, and wildly different ambitions and intentions. The person this article was written about had one thing in common with the person who is writing about her, the name she was born with. Aside from that, the "fingernail bandit" is but a shell of Celeste Wells. 1989 put the proverbial nail in the coffin for the woman who on that particular day was perpetrating a fraud and going by the name Dominica Snyder.

At the time Miami had already become a city of illusions, sunlight and shadows, glamour and hustle at the same time. I learned early how to move between those worlds. Well-dressed, well-spoken, and always three steps ahead, I could walk into any store from South Beach to Aventura and own the room before I even said a word.

By this time, I had been around the world, seen and done more than most women who grew up on my side of town had. By this time, I had created quite a name (31 to be exact) for myself. I and those who knew me, knew a notorious crime queen who dabbled in everything from pimping to drug trafficking. So I didn't expect the moniker I'd go out with to be something so simple as to be known for my long nails with flashy designs and a fake patois accent. Nonetheless, I had surely built a reputation and a legacy of wrongdoing that warranted everything the Miami Herald wrote about me, Celeste Wells, the Notorious fingernail bandit.

It wasn't about greed. It was survival—elevated. A way of navigating a city that offered few legitimate paths for women like me, and even fewer second chances. I understood how to play the game because I never had the privilege of sitting it out.

As far back as I can remember, which was around six years old, I could tell that my life wasn't initially set up to be a good one. In the 60s, Momma would not admit it, but we were poor. It was the 60s, and although she had a college degree, Momma couldn't get a decent job. The best she could do was work in white folks' homes, which was seen by many as a step above slavery. She was lucky to get between eight and ten dollars a day to provide for five kids. As for Daddy, he didn't make much more because he didn't have the education or skills to do so. As a kid, he had to support himself and his family, which meant there was no time for schooling. With only an eighth-grade education there were only so many jobs he could do. He lived a hard life and made sure to make it just as hard for us.

Growing up, I was lucky to get even a couple hours of sleep because I was awakened every night by the sound of Momma screaming as Daddy beat her, one of my siblings, or me. If we woke up to see what was going on we were guaranteed an ass beating; God forbid we try to stop him. It was better to just fake sleep sometimes since Daddy always wanted me to get up and clean his feet, or some other dumb ass chore he demanded and it didn't matter what time it was because if Daddy wanted it - it would have to be done, or he would beat you till you did it. For fear of getting beat, I was always quick about doing what Daddy said, though on the inside, rebelliousness brewed up and grew stronger with every beating and every abusive demand. Since I couldn't stand up to Daddy, and Momma couldn't protect me, that rebelliousness had to find other outlets. My first coping mechanism was not just out of rebelliousness, but also out of lack. Lack of money, love, and the normal things that other kids my age had and did.

The first time I can remember stealing something I was around six years old. I wanted to make Momma happy so I stole some Valentine's Day candy for her. I had been thinking about it all day at bible study. Seeing how upset Momma was with Daddy, and how I couldn't do a single thing about it. I left Bible Study with the same thoughts fresh on my mind the whole way home. By the time I walked into the drugstore, my resolve had hardened enough for me to snatch up a handful of candy without a lick of concern for the consequences.

As quick as I snatched the candy, I got caught, and ran all the way to our house, with the lady from the drugstore running right behind me! When I got home, I had to return the candy and pay my debt to my parents. I got a good beating, which I'm sure they thought had settled me, and my need to misbehave. Little did they know, that getting caught didn't do anything but make me think of how not to get caught the next time and that this was only the beginning. I was a criminal in the making.

Segregation was still in place when I began elementary school. I went to Frank C. Martin In Richmond Heights, Florida. In school, I was a very bright kid. I excelled in all my classes and won spelling contests. Momma said she didn't know where I got my smarts from, because she didn't think much of herself despite her education, and certainly, she didn't think highly of Daddy. Even though I raked in good grades, I had a small behavior problem. The little rebel in me was still there and made me bitter and angry about just about everything. Which I know came from Daddy. He harbored hate like no one and nothing else, and in turn, passed some of that fire down to me. Everyone feared him and like father, like daughter, everyone at school learned to either respect or fear me.

Coming up, I always had a feeling that something about my life would be hard and that I had to fight for mine, so I began trying to make it work my own way. I made myself a leader and decided I would represent my family and friends with my power when they were afraid to stand up for themselves. I was the only one who would say the words I knew they were thinking. For everybody else, it was always, "Yes, ma'am," "No, ma'am," but not Celeste. I had a mouth on me, and if I thought someone wasn't treating me or my friends right, then I'd let them know.

By the time they integrated schools, I was in the fifth grade and was transferred over to Colonial Drive Elementary in the "white section."

That wasn't too bad but we couldn't ride the bus. We had to walk to school up through the woods; with every step I took, all I could think about were the things I hated about my life. What made it worse was that Momma still denied two major things: Daddy's abuse, and us being poor. Here I am walking, getting bit up by mosquitos to sit in a classroom they didn't even want me in. While the white kids rode a bus. I was always tired from walking, and with nothing but time to think it only made me harbor more bitterness and hate for the white folks that made me do it in the first place.

I wasn't born knowing much about white folks. All I knew was that my Auntie hated whites, and with that being all I knew it was sure to be passed right on down to me. Therefore, from "Day One," I went into that white school with a stink eye on every white person that crossed my path.

My first week at Colonial Drive Elementary didn't change the way I viewed whites. In fact, it made it worse. My big fat white teacher, Mr. Wilson, had the nerve to put his hand on me for some reason and I knew that no one but my Momma or Daddy could touch me, and certainly not some fat cracker. I lashed out and hit him back, then ran home back through those same woods I walked through every single morning.

As soon as I got home, I told my Auntie that "Mr. Cracker" put his hands on me. You see, Auntie was someone who nobody wanted to mess with. She was by no means a big woman; at 5'4", she was just barely at a man's chin. However, she made up for her lack of height with her no-nonsense attitude. Auntie would do just about anything to make it known that she wasn't about to be stepped on, not even my uncle could contain her. She took me back to the school and got some straightening done. Now Auntie had enough sense not to pick a fight, but she made it damn clear that nobody would so much as lay a finger on me ever again unless he wanted blood between him and her. Just the look in her eye let him know he shouldn't try to fuck with her.

Whatever she did worked and I never had another problem with him, or any other teacher, for that matter. From that point on, my hate for white people grew. From that point on I held a serious disdain for authority, more specifically, white authority. All I wanted to do was get them back for everything they had done to me and would do to me if I didn't stop them.

For years I carried that quiet rage, a rage that was passed down to me through struggle and memory. I didn't have the words for it back then but I knew it wasn't just about me in a way. It was about how they treated us. So, of course, I wanted revenge. But not the kind that spilled blood, I wanted a different kind of retaliation, the kind that made people uncomfortable just by watching someone like me take up space in places they swore we didn't belong. I walked into stores and those neighborhoods with my head held high and my story is hidden to take what I wasn't "supposed" to have. Not because I didn't know right from wrong, but because I was tired of being told that survival only counted when it followed someone else's rules.

The system never asked me why I felt I had to hustle to eat and live. It never stopped to account for its crimes of generational theft, denied opportunities, and the everyday humiliation that goes into the Black experience. I did what I knew how to do and for a while, it felt like justice. My kind of justice. Flawed, but mine.

CHAPTER 2

The incident with "Mr. Cracker" wasn't the last of my behavior problems at Colonial Drive Elementary. I started getting into fights all the time. One day, we had a talent show and one of the girls wanted to see my breasts. At first, we were only joking around, but then she kept asking and teasing me, making me more and more uncomfortable and I got scared. She persisted until it got physical and I had to fight her off, but in doing so, I broke my front tooth. Now, not only was my tooth chipped I had to explain how it happened. I was afraid because there was no acceptable explanation for my fighting for Daddy. Had he known, not only would I be beaten, but Momma, and whoever else in his path, would have gotten it, too.

Daddy went on a warpath often. The worst time I could remember was when he came home and beat Momma and then stuck her face to the hot stove! It was a moment that I will never forget - I was afraid, defenseless, and unable to stop his violent outbursts against Momma and the rest of us. After seeing that, I knew for sure that I couldn't breathe a word about my fighting. Lord knows if he knew he might've killed Me, Momma, or both of us.

We were ruled through terror, and sometimes I felt like he singled me out because of my rebellious attitude. At least four or five times a week, I could expect Daddy to make me clean his feet early in the morning or something stupid like that. He would come to turn the light on and say,

"Yvonne," (my middle name) and tell me to get up… no one else but me. He would stand there and glare at me, half-naked, with his stuff hanging from the leg of his briefs. Although he never sexually abused me, it was also something I could never put past him.

Because of my trauma and constant living in fear, I sometimes wet the bed. When this happened I had to sleep in the"wash house off the porch" with the dog. I wasn't the only one who was afraid of Daddy, we all lived in fear. One time Momma, Gail (my youngest sister), and I were on the way home in Daddy's truck that he used to transfer clothes from the cleaners where he worked. It was raining hard, so when Momma slammed on the brakes to keep from hitting another car in front of us, we lost control. We ended up flipping over and over, totally destroying the truck, and barely escaping with our lives.

Although we almost all died, we knew that wasn't the end of an already tragic situation, in fact, it was just the beginning. Being hurt in the accident was half of the battle. We were more concerned with what Daddy was going to do to us when he found out about his truck. We thought the worst and feared what seemed like inevitable ass-whoopings. As it turned out, we were right. He was mad but on this particular day, he didn't beat us. He was more concerned about the truck than if we made it out alive. It was only by the grace of God that we were not killed in that accident, and Daddy didn't even seem to care. I guess that was his way of punishing us.

Daddy had a way of putting a damper on just about everything - even Christmas. A lot of the time, we didn't even know when Daddy was going to come home, or what kind of mood he would be in so we always tried to enjoy every moment he wasn't around beforehand. When he arrived, panic mode kicked in; it was almost a guarantee for him to come home fussing and cussing. We just hoped he would fall asleep quick enough for us to salvage what little Christmas cheer we had left.

Momma told us from the start there was no Santa Claus, but I think we knew even before she told us. But it didn't matter much, since we always tried to make the most of what little we could get. I remember we would get a few new things, but the majority came from Goodwill; we had a way of making those old things look good as new. Momma did her best but that wasn't always enough for me, so I resorted to stealing from Goodwill, but not for myself. I would get things for my older sisters just so they could have a few extra goodies, even though they were scared and didn't approve of my actions.

As I got older, I started spending more time away from home, and more importantly, away from Daddy. By the time I was ten years old, I started going to spend the weekends with my "Big Mama," and granddaddy Sam in Liberty City, Florida, which is a thirty-minute drive from Richmond Heights. Sam would make me straddle his leg as I sat on his thigh, which made me uncomfortable, but I never said a word. At least, I got to get away from the drama of being with Daddy. That was until he had to pick me up with Momma - then there was sure to be some type of drama.

Once, he came to pick me up, and he and Momma were really drunk. Before we could turn the corner from Big Momma's house, he had gotten mad and started cursing and hitting on Momma. He then got out of the car and left me and Momma stranded in the car, with no real driver. Poor Momma couldn't see to drive, so it was up to me to get us home. While holding one eye open with her fingers, she said, "Do you see the nose of the car?" I said yes, and then she replied, "You see that line in the middle of the road? Well, keep on the line and take us home." Here I was, a little girl only ten or eleven years old, scared to death with no map, directions, or idea of where I was going with the task of getting us the twenty-eight miles back to the house. Miraculously, though, I did it! When Daddy finally came home, he continued where he left off by beating Momma. While Daddy shouted and Momma cried, all I could think about was counting the days until the next weekend.

I continued to go to Liberty City on the weekends to stay with Big Mama, but I also started staying with Auntie Jeanne. She was Momma's half-sister who lived a block away from us. Every time I was to meet Big Mama for the weekend, we would meet where she worked - which was for white folks. Whenever I went there, I stole everything I could from dirty underwear to their cash. I gave them a little mercy and left them the pennies, though. That went on for as long as I was allowed to go to work with Big Mama.

Even though Daddy never sexually abused me, it still didn't stop other people from trying to take advantage of me. One summer, we were having a family gathering, where I was molested for the first time. My great Uncle sat next to me at the table, and when no one was looking, he snaked his hand under the table, put his hands between my legs, and started penetrating me with his finger. I was more surprised than scared, and though I didn't like it, I didn't know what to do other than just sit there. Even though I was being taken advantage of, something forced me to get some control over the situation. When he finally stopped, I demanded he give me some money, or else I would tell my Daddy what he had done; it turned out as I suspected that just about everyone was afraid of my Daddy. With the fear that my Daddy and everybody else would end up finding out what a nasty old man he was, he ended up giving me some money, I don't recall how much, but I do know it wasn't a lot. What I earned in that situation wasn't the money but the lesson I learned from it. I had just gained knowledge of a valuable skill that would come in handy throughout the rest of my life - the art of manipulation. Knowing the right things to say, and to get what I wanted, also served to protect me from being taken advantage of by others.

Another Uncle tried me once. But when he asked, "Do you tell your Auntie Jeanne everything?" I said yes, knowing he wouldn't want to get caught abusing a little girl. The continued abuse and advances shaped the way I felt about men. Soon, I got used to attracting older men, and I came to expect their advances. The more I matured, the more men would try to make advances on me. But, I never let them get to me, and I always made sure to run to Big Mama's house before anything bad could happen. No one would do that to me again, not if I had anything to say about it.

From then on, I began to sharpen what I saw as a valuable skill: knowing how to navigate situations where I was vulnerable and using my words and instincts to shield myself from harm. It wasn't manipulation as much as it was survival, a defense mechanism to avoid being hurt again. It taught me that while I couldn't always prevent people from crossing boundaries, I could still reclaim some agency in the aftermath.

As I matured, I became accustomed to the attention of older men, often anticipating their advances before they even happened. The more I grew, the more determined I became not to let anyone get the best of me. I learned to listen to my instincts and to seek refuge in places I trusted, like Big Mama's house, before anything bad could happen. Her home was my sanctuary, my safe haven when the world outside felt too dangerous to navigate.

No one would ever cross those lines with me again, not if I had anything to say about it. Those early experiences, painful and unfair, taught me the importance of boundaries, strength, and the ability to protect myself. They shaped not just my survival but also my determination to reclaim power in a world that often tried to strip it away.

CHAPTER 3

By the time I turned fourteen, I started smelling myself. In other words, I started becoming a woman and thinking for myself. This is when I figured out that I didn't have to just sit there and take Daddy's shit. I started to do things without a care in the world for what others would say, much less Daddy. Every night, after my boyfriend's mom headed out to work, I would sneak out of the house, steal the car, and then go so we could have sex at his house right under his mother's nose. I had the whole routine down pat. Once I was done, I quietly pulled back in, snuck up to the window, and then tapped on the glass until Gail, my confidant, would open the door. This went on for quite some time, I was never caught and saw my ability to not get caught as a skill.

With that in mind, stealing cars became another one of my regular habits. Any time my parents had company over, all I could think about was, "How am I going to take their car for a joy ride?" My fingers just itched while I made up plans to pick up their keys that they so stupidly left unguarded on the kitchen table. Too bad, I never stopped to consider the consequences. Instead, I thought, "Screw it," I was slick enough, and I got away with it a few times so how would I possibly get caught? So I would never be caught. However, The more bold I got when I proved myself wrong. My ego didn't do a damn thing to protect me, and eventually my luck ran out. The night I was caught, I was petrified. I got the keys and got as far as starting up the car to find Momma and her friend, Ms. Gloria standing in the middle of the street trying to get me to stop, but I just instead, continued to drive right at them - acting as if I was going to run them over if they wouldn't get out of the way. They eventually moved and I stopped the car. I didn't feel any remorse for trying to take it. I was more upset that they had found out my secret.

Just because I wasn't taking Daddy's shit anymore didn't mean I wasn't still afraid of him. I still minded the rules of his house as much as I could while doing my own thing. Nonetheless, I had places to go in case things got too heated at the house, mainly because I didn't want to take any more beatings. Usually, I would go next door to Ms. Mary's house, which soon became my safe haven from Daddy when he was too dangerous to be around. Whenever I needed a place to stay, she was always there for me. She never let Daddy in, even if he demanded it, and she was just as afraid of him as I was. Ms. Mary was like me and didn't like to hold her tongue. She always got mad at Momma whenever she refused to stand up for herself or retaliate against Daddy. Momma was a very submissive woman, and I hated that she wasn't a fighter. I knew she couldn't help it; Daddy was an intimidating force. Once, I saw him break a windshield with one hand, then turn around, and knock out Mary's husband with the other hand for trying to hold him back from fighting Momma. Even though we knew it was futile, my sisters and I always tried to stand up to Daddy. But Momma, wouldn't even try, which only boiled my blood even more. Sometimes I felt like I had to compensate for all the anger that Momma refused to let out against Daddy, which only made him rain down even harder on me; and as usual, Momma would just stand by silently.

Though I was willing to fight back, fear kept my sisters from doing anything of the sort.

In fact, they were so scared of Daddy that they tried to hide just about everything from him.

When my sister Pam, became pregnant, she kept it hidden right up into her eighth month.

After all, she was just fifteen at the time, and would only be sixteen upon actually giving birth to her son. No one knew she was expecting - not even Momma; Pam wore so many girdles that I lost count. But we knew she couldn't keep it a secret forever and dreaded the day Daddy found out, I thought he would beat that baby right out of her, or worse. Surprisingly, the good Lord smiled down upon my sister the day Daddy found out. For whatever reason he hadn't been drinking that day, and after figuring out that Pam was likely to go into labor in only a few short days, he accepted that he was going to be a grandfather without much cussing and fighting.

Pam was not the only one who had to keep a big secret like that from Daddy. By the time, Pam had her baby; My sisters Debra and Linda were pregnant as well. Debra tried to hide hers too, but Momma figured it out eventually. What was worse, I had gotten pregnant by Randall, making me the fourth girl in the family ready to bring a baby in the house. With all this going on, Momma quickly decided that I was going to have an abortion. I was scared, but I didn't have a choice in the matter. When momma put me in the car, she blindfolded me so I hadn't a clue where we were going. At the time, abortions were illegal so I am sure the blindfolding was to ensure I couldn't identify whoever was doing it. To this day, I am still not sure who it was that stuck some object up my vagina to try to abort the fetus. After the first try, the fetus didn't come down, only a lot of blood. On the second try, something came down: the baby - my baby. Lord knows what they did with that poor mangled-up fetus. Not knowing what happened to my child is something that I often think about, along with where or what my life would have turned out to be had I not gotten the abortion. Linda and Debra went on to have their children, and I was left with nothing but scars. All for the sake of keeping a secret from Daddy.

Today, looking back over some 50 years ago and I'm struck by how little has really changed for women. We're still fighting to control what happens to our own bodies, still battling laws and politicians who want to dictate the most intimate parts of our lives. The same fear I felt then as a little girl. The fear of not having autonomy over my own body, my own baby still to this day hangs heavy in the air. Women's health should never be a political gamble, yet here we are, with rights stripped away and very little access. The struggle for dignity, autonomy, and safety is as urgent now as it was back then, and it's a fight we cannot afford to lose again. Because the cost of losing is not just our bodies, but our freedom, our futures, and our very lives.

As if it wasn't bad enough that my sister was a mother at a young age, the boy who got her pregnant was no good. He turned out to be one of the many guys that would try to take advantage of me. He once gave my friend and me a ride home from the carnival, but after he dropped her off down the street, he continued on, until he passed my house. I asked him where he was going, and he just mumbled incoherently. He ended up going down into this wooded area near the white-folks section. He stopped the car, turned to me, and in a very matter-of-fact commanding voice said, "You know what you gotta do," but he wasn't going to get me so easily. I went berserk: jumped out of the car, and threw a huge rock at the window. It sounded as though I shattered the glass, but I didn't care enough to look to see the damage; I just kept on running. I knew this was the white-folk section, so it was unlikely anyone would help a lost little black girl in the middle of the night, but I was so scared I didn't care. I wanted help and I didn't give a damn who that help came from. I

16

ran from house to house, banging on doors until one of the porch lights came on. I beat at the door, pleading for anyone - someone to help me. A white lady peeked out, but wouldn't let me in. I don't think she thought I was going to rob her, or anything; it's just that during that time, white folk didn't have anything to do with blacks. I kept on banging on the door, until eventually; I just yelled out my Momma's number and begged her to call. Once things got quiet, I gave up for a little bit... I just curled up in a heap and cried outside on that woman's porch. I was just about to get up and start walking; when I saw the lights of our car pull up in the driveway. It turned out that the woman had a heart after all.

Momma was concerned, but scared to let Daddy know what had happened to me. Despite everything, Momma was still worried about getting hurt by Daddy over her own little girl. By this time I had had it; not just with Daddy's abuse, but with every man's abuse. I vowed never to let another man hurt me in any way; ever again, no matter how hard he tried. And, boy did they try.

At that age, I was very physically developed. I had reached full womanhood although I was only fourteen. Men used to tell me, "I'm going to give you another mango season." This was something men would say when a young girl was not quite "ripe" enough for sex. I would just smile because in my mind I knew that I would not let anyone manipulate me; not even Randall, the love of my life. There was a point where I'd become almost a little too aggressive for him, but despite that, he stayed with me. After a while, he just wasn't enough for me anymore. Despite hating abusive men, my new aggressive nature almost demanded that I pick up someone who was more "challenging." Maybe I wanted someone to try to abuse me just so I could have the satisfaction of shooting them down.

After I broke up with Randall, I started going with a boy named Joe, my first "thug," after being with Randall. My friend Marsha introduced us when we were hanging out at Coconut Grove. Girls from the Heights loved the boys from the Grove, and Joe fit the bill. Joe and his friends used to ride around in stolen cars all the time, which just attracted me even more. I remember Joe and I having sex upstairs in the back of the school. During that time, it was common to do it in the back of a car, or wherever else Joe felt like. Sadly, Joe and I didn't get to stay together as long as I would have liked.

Growing up, I could dance my ass off and was always participating in talent shows at school. Everybody wanted to see my group and I dance. One day, not long after Joe and I started seeing each other, he and his boys were riding around in a stolen car. In fact, all of us had been riding around in the same car earlier that day, before the talent show, including Joe's little sister, Sapphire, who was performing in the show with us. When the show was over, we caught wind that the police had killed Joe. The police tried to get the boys to pull over, and like idiots, they drove faster to try and outrun the police. Eventually, the boys stopped the car, but when the police came up to the car, they said that Joe had something in his hand; it turned out to be nothing more than a pen or something stupid like that. Joe was killed, one boy was shot in the leg, and the others got away. Even though Joe was riding around in a stolen car, the Miami Police Department settled out of court with Joe's family for his death. For the times we lived in, an out-of-court settlement and the police conceding to their wrongdoing was a big deal. They've been killing us without remorse for years. The fact that although he had no business in a stolen car, they still understood that he didn't deserve to die meant a lot. His family was at least given the peace of mind that it was an accident and that spoke volumes. I, along with everyone else was shocked at that notion.

After Joe died, I was emotionally destroyed because it was the first time I had ever experienced the death of someone that close. After all, I had been with him earlier that day, and he was even supposed to pick us up from the talent show. I couldn't believe that he was gone – dead – never coming back. I attended the funeral, and Momma stood by my side the whole time. She said she felt my pain and even showed sympathy for me. However, after the funeral was over, she showed her true colors, as I encountered a rather unpleasant personal hygiene situation. I jumped in the shower immediately upon returning home from the funeral, because for some reason I felt itchy as hell. Despite scrubbing and scrubbing, the itch wouldn't go away, so I called Momma in to tell her. When she came in, she took one good look and said that I had crabs. She screamed at me and called me every dirty name in the book. Even though hours earlier she was crying right beside me and being compassionate. I can look back and laugh about this now, but at the time, I was not only sad about Joe's death, but also furious over the fact that Momma had turned on me so quickly after being so kind to me. Nevertheless, I was too tough to let anything bother me any longer than it needed to. Even though I had suffered a loss, I bit back my tears and continued down my path of rebellion and ultimate self-destruction.

CHAPTER 4

Coming up without much money in a house full of girls made it difficult to always be able to afford the things my friends had but like any teenage girl, I always wanted to look good for myself and especially for boys. My best friends, Marsha and Phyllis were well off. Their mother and father owned both a convenience store and a record store. They were able to get just about anything and everything they ever wanted. I had the looks but didn't have the clothes, shoes, and money to keep up with myself like they did and that put a little pressure on me. My family and I had a hard enough time getting the things we needed, that we couldn't even consider going out to get the things we wanted. This put a burning desire in me to get it the best way I could. Lack motivated me to figure it out. Soon I learned that I could "earn" money to have just as much as my friends had, regardless of how I "earned" it. I wasn't a stranger to light shoplifting, and by the time I was a teen, I had enough nerve to sneak more than just a handful of candy and a pack of gum. What started as a quick fix quickly turned into an addiction. My palms literally itched every time I walked into a store. I became blind to the price tags; they were no longer a limiting factor. As far as I was concerned, I could afford whatever I could smuggle out unnoticed. Soon I was sharing the glories of the five-finger discount with my friends, who turned out to be just as keen on stuffing their pockets as I was.

I convinced a friend of mine, Cynthia, to go shoplifting with me at Zayre's, a popular department store back then. I was no stranger to the store either, especially since my sisters and I made a regular habit of stealing from them. I figured that eventually the owners might get a little suspicious of me, so my friend and I decided to go in "undercover." We borrowed a couple of her mom's wigs and, thinking that we were completely inconspicuous, headed inside the store. After we had finished stealing and were almost out of the store, I heard a man stop Cynthia. My throat went dry and for a split second, I felt as if lightning had struck me on the spot. Despite how scared I was, I couldn't stop my legs from carrying me away from the scene. I kept going - I mean I was moving fast. I did not give Cynthia a second thought... after all; she was dumb enough to get caught. Why should we both go down? Suddenly, I heard Cynthia say, "Celeste, Come on! You got some too!" I cursed and moved quicker, but the man still managed to catch up, grab hold of my arm, and take me back to the scene. He sat the two of us down so that he could go call the cops. When they took us down to the station and asked for our parent's numbers, I didn't speak. I was scared to call my Momma since there was a chance that Daddy was somewhere close. Cynthia's Momma came to get her hours before I finally cracked, and gave the cops my number.

Momma stormed into the station just minutes after they called her. What a sight I must have been. There I was, fifteen years old and looking like I was twenty, tear-stained face, hidden under a cheap, lopsided wig and seated between two cops. Momma took me right home for a good beating. I shed some tears and promised to behave, over and over, until Momma got tired of beating me - convinced that she had knocked all of the disobedience right out of me. She demanded that I leave Cynthia alone. Momma didn't even consider that I was the one who talked Cynthia into the whole thing. It was then that I realized how much power I had. Not even Momma could see through my lies anymore. Moreover, just like I was willing to leave Cynthia to take all the blame, I was willing to give an empty promise to Momma. From that point on, I just retraced where we went wrong and perfected my "craft." Anytime I went into a store after that day, I stole something. Stealing wasn't always about satisfying myself. I always made sure to look out for my family, and I did my best to get my sisters and my Momma all the little things that they couldn't get on their own. My sisters looked down on me for stealing, but it didn't matter what they thought. None of my sisters had the heart that I had; they wouldn't even attempt to do the things I did. Whenever we went to Goodwill, I always made sure to sneak a little extra for everyone. One time we went to the store and I convinced my sisters to distract Momma long enough for me to nab some shoes for her.

Pretty soon Goodwill wasn't enough for me anymore. Momma and the rest of the family deserved better, and I loved the thought of getting my hands on more valuable items. Once I got bolder, I started going to small boutiques. I would roll up the clothing very tightly and tuck it between my legs. From there I would carefully move out to the car, deposit my goods, then return and repeat the process until I was completely satisfied. I became so skilled at my routine that I started getting greedy for more. I finally moved up to Jordan Marsh, which was like Saks Fifth Avenue to me. Long story short: the more I stole, the more I wanted to; the risk became part of the reason why I stole. I loved the thrill. The more expensive the store, the more of a thrill I got from stealing their stuff. It wasn't long before I started smuggling out name-brand clothing beneath my own tattered clothes. Each time I walked out I left with whatever my heart desired and without a hint of remorse.

Momma had a good heart and saw the best in everyone so she couldn't imagine her daughter being a thief. She always did her best to instill good qualities in all of us, and to assure us that no matter how poor we were, we would never need to stoop so low that we had to steal. But poverty was hard and seeing people with more than we had while I struggled seemed unfair. I didn't have the will or the means to listen to any more of her lectures. Once I had gotten a taste of stealing, it was almost impossible for me to stop. If Momma ever did have any real knowledge about my stealing, it didn't matter. Still, she never gave up on me.

Keeping it from Momma wasn't that hard, but Daddy was a different story. He never had a clue about my stealing; I always tried hard not to run into him, or give him any reason to suspect me. I hid everything as soon as I brought it home. Sometimes, even, I would store things at Aunt Mary's house for a few days, then come home with the new clothes and lie and say I bought them while I was with Auntie. Marsha and Phyllis provided a good excuse for any new clothing as well. They always had new clothes, so whenever Daddy would ask about anything he hadn't seen before; I would say that I borrowed it from them. Marsha knew about my stealing, so I used her as a cloak whenever I went shopping. It always helped when someone was spending cash while I stole, that way the storekeepers were less suspicious of me. My friend, Brenda, knew I was stealing as well, and even though she disagreed with it, she had enough money to buy her own things, so she didn't care if I occasionally slipped something into my pocket.

My sister, Gail, was the only one who did not care for my stealing at all. Funnily enough, though, Pam and Linda didn't agree with it, but they never turned down any gifts I had for them. It was ironic, whenever I went out, they always had something to say, calling me a thief and a liar for going behind Momma's back yet the second I got home, they always waited with wide eyes and searched my bags for anything in their size. As far as they were concerned, as long as their hands were not dirty, there was no reason to turn down my generosity. This taught me that there were many people like them in the world who, although they would never commit the crimes themselves, had no problems benefiting from the misdeeds of others.My sisters kept their hands clean, their noses high, and their morals right where they believed they should be. But the lights stayed on, we kept clothes, and sometimes that extra treat or gift found its way into their hands because of things I did. And while they didn't always approve of how it was done, they didn't ask either.I don't say that to throw shade. I say that, to tell the truth about how survival works. We were all trying to make it, each in our own way.

Some of us followed the rules, and some of us had to make up our own. That doesn't make one path better than the other, just different. They didn't judge me with malice in their hearts, and I didn't offer my help expecting gratitude. We were sisters, raised in the same house under the same roof of fear and lack. They tried to keep their dignity intact, and I tried to keep afloat. That's just the way it was. I never held it against them that they looked at me sideways sometimes — and I hoped, deep down, they never held it against me that I did what I had to do.

CHAPTER 5

Everybody in my soon-to-be crew shared the same qualities as I did, as well as similar upbringings. My best friends, Charlotte and Shirley were two sisters out of a family of ten siblings. Their mother was bed-ridden most of the time, so her children had to fend for themselves. Naturally, they all had to cheat a little to survive, so hustling was a common game for Charlotte and Shirley. Through them, I met Mary, a girl who already knew how to hold her own. She knew how to dress, how to act, and played the game like a pro. I admired her skill, and through her, refined some of my own. I was not easily impressed but I took a liking to how she carried herself.. Mary earned my respect by sporting a flashy Cadillac, one I shamelessly took out from time to time, without her knowing. Kim was the weak link of the group. Even though she wasn't much of a thief, I had known her since grade school, which made me feel safe around her, especially when things got too heavy with the rest. I had to stand up for her more than once, but had I not known her for so long, I might have turned her out of the group from the very start.

My crew and I made a name for ourselves quickly… We weren't just a bunch of regular thieves; we knew how to pull it off with some class. We only dressed in the finest clothes and spoke so well that shopkeepers couldn't see what was behind our flashy smiles. People might not have known our names, but they damn sure knew who we were. Whenever a store was cleaned out, everyone knew who was behind it, "Those girls from down south." What fueled us was, the more our reputation grew, the more notorious and audacious we got.

Charlotte and I went to a local football game one night and, as always, she was dressed to capture attention. In fact, she was bordering on the line of looking like a high-class prostitute that night. Of course, we were all showing some flesh, so it wasn't hard for us to turn a few heads. To be honest, we didn't give a damn about the game; we had a different agenda that night. We batted our eyes and showed off our clothes, which were fresh off the racks from some of our favorite boutiques. Our five-finger discount had us looking like money. Whenever a guy would get up enough nerve to come close, or better yet, speak to us, we'd shoot him down so quickly, he didn't even have time to feel the whiplash. It was all just a tease – and a game I was quickly learning to love.

After the game, we went to Royal Castle, a burger joint where everyone hung out. It turned out Charlotte had brought back an admirer from the game who happened to be a white guy. At first, we all ignored him as he made obvious advances at Charlotte. When it became obvious he wasn't going to leave her alone, we decided to take advantage of the situation. Charlotte invited him into the car and kept him busy in the backseat while the rest of us discussed what to do with him. Then, we noticed some other guys from the game, so we decided to let them in on the plan. They got into the trunk of the car, and we left and parked near the canal. Just as the white guy thought he was going to get lucky with Charlotte, the guys jumped out of the trunk, beat him, and stole his money. It turned out that he only had a couple of hundred dollars for us to split up. Irritated, one of the guys threw the man in the canal and left him for dead. That night was the first of many experiences that gave me a sense of the dangerous game I was playing and where my life was heading.

Shoplifting was becoming far less of a tame experience for me, as well as for the people around me. On one of my shoplifting excursions with Charlotte, we invited my sister, Linda to come along with us since she had a car. On our way out of the store, we noticed that a detective was trailing close behind us.

Under normal circumstances, we might have just run, but Linda had a different idea; as the detective approached to question us, she turned and attacked him! Caught completely off guard, the detective went to the ground, with my sister on top of him, clawing at his face. Charlotte and I were dumbstruck, but at the first sound of sirens, our only thought was to run, so we didn't even consider trying to pull Linda off the man. After all, it didn't make sense for all of us to go to jail. When I got home, I had to find some way to tell Momma that Linda was locked up for assaulting an officer. Even though the merchandise we had gotten away with was worth more than Linda's bail, I didn't want to hint to momma that I might have been stealing. There was no way I was going to get dragged down like Linda. As a result, I let her sulk, mad as hell, in jail for the night, guilt gnawing at my gut, but my resolve was as hard as ever.

As I approached my late teens, my friends and I had developed our shoplifting into a regular routine. We would get up early in the morning and meet up after feeding our parents stories about where we were going. I usually told Momma I was out looking for a job. Our crew consisted of Shirley, Charlotte, Mary, and me. Charlotte still hadn't perfect not getting caught and wasn't that good of a thief, so she served more as the distraction girl. While she kept a shopkeeper busy, we would make several rounds in and out of the store, taking turns so no one would get suspicious of us constantly returning. We would also go to the mall and exit the back door with an arm full of clothes; we were most likely the reason why stores began to lock up their back doors. When I got home, I usually stashed my goods out back by a big tree where I would pick them up later. Then, if I ever wanted to sneak out at night, I would just tell my sister, Gail, that I was going out and to open the door when I got back.

Soon stealing became less about the clothes and more about the challenge. Sometimes I wouldn't even look at what I was stealing; I would just glance at the price tag to see what it was worth. I remember the day I spotted a golden metallic outfit on a mannequin. It was the very same that my idol Foxy Brown usually wore. I wanted that outfit so damn bad. While inside we looked for other outfits the same as the one on the mannequin, but the only one they had left was on the mannequin. Despite that, I wasn't about to leave without the outfit. As a distraction, I wound up getting in a fight with the woman in the store. While I wrestled with her, one of my friends grabbed the mannequin while the others took the money from the register. We got away, but it turned out that the suit didn't even fit me. That incident became so well known that many boutiques changed their entrances so that the only way to get in was for a store clerk to buzz you in.

Life was moving fast for me and all I wanted was what I perceived as the "fabulous life." As a result, I grew arrogant of my abilities. I thought there wasn't a person in the world who could outsmart, out-steal, or out-manipulate me. One day, that mentality almost changed. Kim and I were walking down the street and met up with a guy named Daryl, who was probably around eighteen years old. Now, it wasn't Daryl who caught my eye it was his clothes, and his brand new Caddy that quickly earned my affection. I still had a weak spot for nice cars, and against our better judgment, Kim and I got in the car with him. He said something about going to see his father, but without even mentioning where his father lived.

As we rode, the hours seemed to be going by quickly as they jumped from two to ten. By now, Kim and I were a little nervous, but we were too far from home to make any kind of complaint. We got hopeful the first time he stopped, but after a second couple joined us in the car, we knew we were stuck. Every time we stopped, the couple got out to con some poor sucker on the street out of a couple thousand dollars. By the time they could figure out what hit them, we had already driven off. We stopped several more times, and each time they would hit a lick. We were all the way in Pensacola by the time Daryl stopped and got us a room. He never let us in on his plans but soon we realized just what the plans he had for us were. Maybe if he had the right approach, he may have been successful in getting me to do what he wanted but once I caught wind of it I knew we were not on the same page. He was trying to pimp us out but unfortunately for him, being a whore was not one of my hustles.

Daryl told me that the only way that I was going to get home was if I turned some tricks, but I would be damned if I let that happen. Nevertheless, I was running out of options. I was caught between turning into a whore and letting my Momma know where I was. To be honest, at that point, I wasn't sure of what was worse. However, the idea of turning tricks for some man, or worse, some cracker, made me sick enough to swallow my pride and call Momma. That day, I was the lucky one; Momma paid for a one-way bus ticket home, but Kim's mom refused to come to her rescue. I think poor Kim had to do what I wouldn't to get her ticket home. Daryl was the first man to try to turn me over to "the life," and unfortunately he wasn't going to be the last.

CHAPTER 6

My little misadventure with Daryl didn't do a thing to curb my interest in men who were bad for me. At seventeen, I felt I was ripe, ready, and hungry for a man. My young impressionable mind had already been groomed to think that's what I needed. Older men had me associating them with money and that's what caught my eye more than anything else did, though, which is why I met up with Booker T. He may have been well into his forties, but he looked damn good. Not only was he handsome, but he knew how to impress a lady. He swept me off my feet with his wining and dining, and of course, that brand spanking new Cadillac. Because I was a schoolmate with his sons, Momma wasn't too suspicious of Booker T., at least, not early on. When Momma started asking me about him, I would just say he was someone who gave us a ride. After all, he was just a nice man with a good job at the airport. But, after she saw him hanging on me just a little too close and one time too many she finally confronted me about it. She said firmly that if she saw this man on me one more time, she would call the police. But there was no way I was going to let my mother get in the way I liked Booker T. too much. Consequently, I had to get creative and find other ways to meet him. While I may have been worried about Momma getting in the way, Booker T was far more concerned about Daddy getting wise to our relationship. I had to assure him numerous times that Momma would never tell Daddy for fear of what he might do to her and me let alone him.

Still, fear of my father kept Booker T. from pushing the envelope, and from that point on, he only would pick me up several blocks away from the house. By now, I was smoking a lot of weed, which was rather lightweight stuff in the scheme of things. Booker T. preferred the hardcore stuff, like angel dust, cocaine, and heroin. He always offered it to me, and I tried it occasionally. But, I must say, it wasn't my cup of tea. I knew that if I was high I wouldn't be able to handle my business, and I preferred having my wits about me. Being out of control of my own body was too disturbing a thought for me to use drugs regularly. Thankfully, Booker wasn't all about drugs. As a man, he knew how to please a lady he proved to be more than enough for me to handle in the bedroom. But, as much fun as Booker T. was, I eventually outgrew him, and of course, it didn't take long for me to meet someone else. Another older man, because by this time I had settled on the idea that someone older is what was needed to keep up with me.

Not only was Horace Williams older but he was also a married man. He lived a few doors down from my sister, Linda. I would see him coming and going on occasion, but he was so back and forth I wasn't too sure if he actually lived at his house. It didn't take me long to figure out that he was a thief. His reputation named him as one of the best in southern Florida. Like Booker T., he was a heroin and coke junkie. As much as I disliked drugs, I knew it was something that came with the territory. As soon as I saw the white El Dorado he rolled in, I looked past the drugs and hopped my ass right into that car!

While I was with Horace, I met a girl named Donna. She was a lot younger than I was which just proved that hard times don't discriminate. I could remember being her age and wondering if my small home and town was all life had to offer so I saw something in her and took her under my wing. Even though she was just fifteen, she was one hell of a thief, and perfect for my crew. Donna and I had more in common than some sisters did. When I saw her, I saw myself, the same rebellious kid struggling against a world that kicked her down at every opportunity... hell, we even looked alike. We even shared the same terrible taste in men; as far as I was concerned, she and I were both in the same boat and cut from the same cloth.. Unlike me, though, Donna could never quite dig her way out of the darker side of life. Later on in life, I found out that her own brother shot her to death. I never did find out why her brother pulled that gun on her, all I know, was that it should have ended differently. What happened to poor Donna was just some sick sin against God - she never even had the opportunity to turn her life around.

Perhaps, if I had had a little more insight back then, and knowing what I know now, I might not have let myself sink so far down either. At the time, though, I was ignorant and uncaring for the consequences of my actions, so my life continued with reckless abandon.

I don't know what kind of stamp I had on my forehead, but I continued to attract and run into controlling, manipulative, and of course, older, men. I met a guy they called Tallyho in Perrine through another friend of mine. He worked at the port as a longshoreman, so I knew he made a lot of money. He fell long, hard, and deep for me. His money and good looks helped me overlook the fact that he was a good 20 years older than I was. But, it was just a little harder to overlookhis controlling nature. Tallyho did his damndest to shape me into some perfect little puppet of his, and for a time, I played along. It's not that I wanted to, of course, but fear has a way of keeping you in check. He provided me with tailored clothing, the matching outfits to go with his, of course. He even started giving me weed to sell, which I did, but it held no thrill for me.

Tallyho let everyone know that I was his girl and that he wasn't playing. I hadn't a clue why, but he really felt like he had something special with me. With me, though, it was never so serious. I knew he wanted me, but I wanted whom *I* wanted, not who wanted me. At the time, I was quite the looker, which made Tallyho's jealousy ten times worse. One night, unfortunately, I learned just how dangerous his jealousy could be. I returned home late after forgetting to let Tallyho know that I was going to be out. He was sitting at home, waiting with whiskey on his breath and murder in his eyes... just like Daddy.

He accused me of running around on him when I was only over at my sister's house. I did my best to calm him down, but he refused to believe me. Without warning, he advanced on me and proceeded to beat me with some clothes hangers. Thankfully, my pride ended up more injured than my body. After that incident, I knew immediately that this would be the last time he would get a chance to put his hands on me. He was too much like my father - trying to use fear to keep me in check. I was far too familiar with that game, and I knew how dangerous it could end up if I played along. Soon after, I eased out of his grasp, I figured out that Tallyho wasn't just talking smack, he intended to back up every threat he made against me. It hadn't even been a minute since we had stopped seeing each other when he rolled up and demanded to talk to me. I was at a club/bar called the Cab Stand, enjoying the music and having a good time; the last person I expected to see was him. Reluctantly, I agreed to speak to him, since I figured it'd be safe in a public place; he and I walked to the side of the building. The second we were out of view, he immediately started pulling me around into the alleyway. I was scared to death, especially when he made the statement, "I'm gonna do you just like I did that other "bitch." My thoughts raced back to our previous scuffles, where he had mentioned another girl that he had done in for crossing him. Pinned up against that wall with Tallyho's hands around my neck, I quickly figured out it might not have just been tough talk. "*Oh hell no,*" I thought to myself, I am not about to die like this. I began

36

to fight him like crazy. I screamed at the top of my lungs, but no one could hear me over the music inside. All my yelling must have made him edgy though, because he let go for a second. By the grace of God, I was able to get away from him.

I might have been able to escape imprisonment from all of my cons, not to mention being almost strangled to death by Tallyho, but karma eventually caught up to me in the most ironic of twists. I was at my mom's house relaxing, when all of a sudden I doubled over as blinding pain struck me right in my groin. Momma was working, and I was in too much pain to call for her. I can't quite remember who was at home with me, but they took me to Coral Reef Hospital, where my life would change forever. Nobody told me a word about what was wrong until after I was under the knife. When I woke up, they informed me that I had required an emergency hysterectomy. For a minute, I couldn't breathe, think, or move. There I was, just seventeen years old, without a thing in the world, and now with no hope of having a family of my own. Everything was gone, just like that, leaving me with one question… why? The doctor muttered something about my ovary and a bad appendix, but I knew the real reason. That botched abortion and all my fucking around with Tallyho had ruined me. What made it worse was that Momma swore me into secrecy once again. Me being barren was bad enough but here I was left to suffer in silence. It was like I had a scarlet letter on me that only I could see and only Momma knew about. My world had crumbled around me in less than a day, and I didn't even have the freedom to grieve about it without risking even more pain.

After going through rehab, I was still staying at Momma and Daddy's place. Despite having had a long overdue dose of reality, I kept living life just as I had before. I didn't take my surgery very seriously, so within a day I was moving around as usual. I was even willing to let guys have me. The way I figured, nothing else was going right, so, why let a littlesurgery get me down? I kept on with my daily hustle - trying to find myself, as I pretended. All I really wanted to do was look good, dress to impress, stack my dough, and flirt with the guys. But, thanks to good ole' Daddy, as well as my previous experiences, I was still not about to become any man's slave bitch. It was going to be about me or it wasn't going to be about anything.

A childhood friend of mine and I started hanging out in this area called, "The Swamp." The Swamp was a safe haven for all the lowlifes of Overtown; Hustlers, Pimps, and Jamaicans, fresh off the ships, all gathered at The Swamp, which made it a perfect place for my crew and me. Overtown was not a place that just anyone wanted to visit, it was "the other side of the bridge" and a far cry from what folks loved about the rest of South Florida. Most people would rather travel through the pits of hell than go anywhere near Overtown. You could be robbed blind, and beaten half to death before you even got a chance to wince. I guess I had the nerve because, despite the danger, I liked going there.

Through a friend of my friend, I met a guy named Stocking; I knew the second I met him that he liked me. He was not a handsome kind of guy, but he had a suave way about himself; plus, he possessed the bonus package - he was a hustler. He sold weed, and I mean lots of it. While I still didn't have a taste for drugs, it was never to the point where I didn't want the money that came with it. Stocking raked in plenty from his "business."

Sometimes, I would go into his apartment and have to walk over huge trash bags full of dope; it was a wonder how he kept himself out of jail sometimes. Stocking lived in an apartment down the street from a bar called "Merlin's." Like most of my relationships, Stocking was more into me than I was into him. He had love for me, but as before, he was just another toy for me. If it wasn't for his particular situation, I might have taken him more seriously. He had jumped ship from Jamaica while working on a cruise ship as a chef. Once he got off, he never got back on. It didn't take very long for him to tell me he loved me enough to marry me, but I was a little suspicious of just what kind of love he was talking about - love for me, or love of the idea of obtaining his citizenship. Still, he had potential, so I tried to hang in there.

After my hysterectomy, having sex with him was almost impossible. It was unbearable and very uncomfortable. However, since he was taking care of me so well, I always found ways to see past the pain. Not only did he take care of me financially, but also he could cook, clean, and do just about everything I needed him to do while I just sat around and watched him. Most people feared Stocking, but, thankfully, I never had a reason to. In all the time he and I were together, he never put a hand on me. Of course, he would get angry at times, but he always gave me fair warning to get out of his way. When he would get mad, he would just say, "Go on and go hay…" which meant, "Get the hell out of my face."

Stocking would go on to become one of Miami's notorious gangsters. They called him and his crew the "Shower Posse," but to me, he was still just Stocking. During his gangster reign, he even made it on *America's Most Wanted* - they wanted to question him about twelve unsolved murders. I loved being around him because I felt safe around him, he always made me feel good even though other people feared him and I both liked and needed that type of security.

As good as Stocking was to me, I eventually left him for one of his partners, Winston (Winnie Reed) -Stocking's supplier. One day, he saw me at Stocking's joint, took one look at me, and said, "Let's go, ma." Winston was on the short side,compared to me, but his furious power made up for his stature. He was the type of person who meant what he said. He said he and I were going to take a ride somewhere, and we never returned. Just that fast he made me his woman.

39

On our way out, we stopped by his house, and he told me to wait in the car. While I waited in the car, I could hear a lot of commotion in the house. All of a sudden, there was the sound of a gunshot. I turned white and instinctively reached for the door handle, but quickly decided against running, once I saw him coming back. He calmly walked out the door, got in the car, and coolly began to explain to me that he had just shot his wife in the leg because she was being disrespectful. This blew me away, because not only did he just shoot someone, but also because I didn't even know the man was married. He knew he couldn't go back to his place, since the police would be looking for him, so we sought refuge over at his friend, King Sporty's place who was a reggae musician. King Sporty later went on to marry the Queen of Soul from Miami, Betty Wright.

What started out as a day or two quickly turned into a few months. The whole time I was with him, I felt locked up. The man watched my every move; I couldn't sneeze without him jumping on me. The way he saw it, he loved me so much and felt he could do whatever he wanted. For a small-sized man, many people feared him, which included Stocking, and even me, sometimes. He didn't want me looking at anyone but him, and he meant it. One night we were at the T.T. Green Night Club on 22nd Ave. This was in the early 70s, so, of course, everybody knew him since he had already made a name for himself. Anyway, I was sitting at the bar as he was making his rounds in the club, but he kept watching me to see what I was doing. I was having drinks, minding my business, and looking pretty in a purple chiffon dress that he had bought for me. A gentleman approached me and asked if I was with someone. I said yes, but Winston saw us talking and immediately became angry. He took me in the back and literally beat my ass. I was so mortified I didn't even have enough sense to fight back or run. We drove home in silence, and as I went inside to nurse my battered body and pride, he had the nerve to ask to make love to me. I told myself that I didn't want to live like this. I started spending all my time contemplating how I was going to ditch him, because I couldn't take that kind of "love" and abuse. I had seen this kind of "love" my whole life. Momma had gotten enough for all of us and I wasn't about to repeat the cycle. Still, I knew if I left him, I couldn't be seen around town anymore. No one would be able to protect me, because Winston feared no one.

My return home was bittersweet. Of course, Momma and Daddy welcomed me home with open arms, but I could see that I had put Momma through hell with worry. They didn't question me much as to where I had been, since I told them I had been staying with Donna the whole time. Lying had become so easy that I even started to believe that's where I was the whole time, if only to make it easier on myself. When I returned home, I had an even bigger appetite for some real money. Within just a few days, an opportunity all but crashed at my feet.

Kim and I had heard about this club called the "Galaxy" on 79th Street and found out that they were having a Mack Ball, an affair where pimps and hoes from all around the country would get together for an annual reunion. You would see all sorts of Caddies, stretched limos, furs, pinky rings, diamonds, and jewels of all sorts. All we could think about was allthose fine, not to-mention rich men. It was as if we had died and gone to Ghetto Heaven. We spent hours getting ready. I sported a fly outfit I got from a high-end boutique, called Noah's Ark; it was a patchwork jean outfit, worth well over a thousand dollars. I found a matching hat and some fly shoes. I sported my reddish blonde hair, accented the outfit with pink earrings, and a scarf. From there, I was off to make my entrance. I was 18 years old, and with those heels, I stood 6'1. I knew I was looking good and for once in my life, I didn't feel out of place. I was ready for the games to begin.

Kelly boasted the title of Mr. Mack, himself. The now famous pimp, Don Magic Juan couldn't even touch Kelly; Kelly had about ten girls in his stable and they weren't your regular cheap hookers, though; every girl was polished and well respected. Even though he was a bona fide pimp, Kelly and I became fast friends -much to the dislike of his whores. While Kelly was plenty fine, Billy was something else. He was a fly dresser, and he knew how to get the ladies' attention and most certainly mine. Before the night was over, he gave me his number, and told me that he was staying at the Holiday Inn, then invited me to go to Kelly's after-party at Kelly's house; hell, I thought that was a great privilege especially since I had never seen or experienced anything like that before. At the same time, fear knotted up my stomach. I was young, fine, in my prime and amongst pimps. A rib-eye in a tiger cage. It was no doubt that a man like this would try to turn me. Even with that in mind, I wasted little time letting Billy know that yes, I would be attending the after-party with him.

Initially, I had banked on clinging to Kim for a good portion of the party, but after meeting a guy named Fritz, she left me and hung out with him. I didn't stay at the party too long because Billy had other things in mind. We went back to the hotel, and he made love to me - making me feel like I had never felt before. The way he touched each part of my body, let me know that he was not an amateur which would probably explain one of the reasons why he was such a good pimp. Being a good lover fit right into his job description which was to manipulate women into doing what he wanted them to do. He acted as if he wanted me to be his woman, but I knew good and damn well, that the whole time he was just trying to recruit me. I didn't mind though. I let him wine and dine with me at the most exclusive spots, let him give me wonderful gifts, and took whatever else he was offering. At eighteen, I was still hiding the darker reality of my life from my parents. Whenever Billy came and got me, it would always be from the corner; my father would have killed us both if he had come to the door. Like most of the men I got with, he was good to me, but there was always a catch of some kind. I still was no fan of "the life" but I knew better than to protest.

One night after dinner, Billy took me to Biscayne Blvd to make a few stops. He made his first stop where the prostitutes hang out. He stopped and picked up this white girl named Sunny. She jumped in the back seat of his car and immediately laid down. Back in those days if a black man was seen with a white girl they would be stopped, especially a pimp who was riding around in a white-on-white Sedan Deville Brougham. Billy said something to her, she gave him a wad of money, and then he let her out. He continued on a bit further down the street and stopped again, where this black girl named Cynt was standing. You could tell she was a real young girl. She didn't hesitate to give him money, either. While I was fascinated, it still wasn't quite enough to tempt me. Billy still had not asked me to do anything, but I knew it was just a matter of time. After he dropped me off that night, I didn't contact him for a while.

I began to miss Billy and his good loving and found myself thinking back to the last time I saw him. But I knew one thing for sure is that I didn't want to be a prostitute even though seeing him wave so much cash in front of me was worse than tempting a junkie with a fresh needle. Perhaps, that was his plan all along; as I'm sure, he knew it would be just a matter of time before my cravings set in. Finally, after a few months, I called him. I needed another dose of the glamorous life. As expected, Billy came to pick me up, only this time he felt bold enough to come to my house and wait for me to come out. I nearly had a heart attack when I heard his engine revving right outside. Daddy was in the living room and saw the white caddy when it pulled up. He immediately went outside and told him to get his ass out in front of his house. I was scared to death, and

I was ready to go, but Daddy made him get off the street. I was looking out the window and could see him circling the other street.

As I contemplated sneaking out, I felt my heart clench up once again, but not from fear. Was I really willing to sneak out with a pimp right from under Daddy's nose? A few minutes ticked by, but I knew what was going to happen, even before I snuck out the back door. I cut through the yard and flagged Billy down. With a big silly grin on my face, I hopped into the passenger seat of the car, oblivious to the fact that this would be one of the biggest mistakes of my life. It was on that day that I left home for good, eighteen years old with my first pimp.

CHAPTER 7

From the first day I was back with Billy, he let me know exactly what it was. He didn't waste a second before he began breaking the "life" down to me. I told him I was a booster, not a whore, and I preferred to keep it that way. As far as I knew, we had an agreement, so I let him begin teaching me the ropes. He sent me out with his white girl, Sunny, to Miami Beach. She knew I didn't want to trick, so she tried to show me how to *pretend* that I was sucking dick. I had the saliva, and the head and hand game going, like I was really doing something. At the same time, I would be putting my hands in John's pocket. By the time we were working at the Newport Hotel down on Collins Beach, I had mastered the game. The set-up was simple: Sunny would go in with John; I would wait a few minutes, then knock and say I needed to use the bathroom. When I pretended to go into the bathroom, I turned off the lights, turned on the water, and then came out to get John's pants and remove the wallet. The first time, I almost managed to complete the task and get away without a hitch, but it was a two-part job. I was no rookie at stealing, but doing it at the same time as trying to turn a trick was like jumping rope and chewing bubble gum, it took practice. Just when I thought I had the routine down pat, my adrenaline started rushing, and I got a little too excited about what I was doing. I forgot about finishing the job according to the plan. Once I finally got my hands on the wallet, I immediately jetted out the door.

I refused to turn tricks but Sunny and Billy tried to convince me otherwise. I didn't care how convincing they tried to be, I was determined not to become a prostitute. I was a thief, end of story. We decided that my job would remain the same. I would create a scene with another girl so that the John was distracted long enough for me to steal his money. After we worked out some of the kinks, our new con worked out perfectly. I was learning the game so fast that it started to feel as though I was meant for this type of lifestyle straight from the womb. My attitude had changed very little over the years; I still wanted to be the best at anything and everything I did. Just like with everything else, I practiced perfecting my hustle game. Before long, I had built a reputation for myself. Soon, everyone knew who I was, and I proudly wore my label of the "baddest bitch" in the business. I basked in all the attention. Whores from other stables either shot dirty looks of jealousy or begged at my feet for a pointer or two. Every pimp that crossed my path wanted a piece of me, but they didn't know that I wasn't going to be just anybody's girl. Being top dog meant that I could be selective about who I chose to be with, and as long as I was the number one bitch, I played along.

By now, Billy was pretty much letting me do whatever I wanted. Even though he still had to lay the pipe with his other girls to keep them happy, he still found ways to show me that it was all about me. He gave me much more quality time, and always overlooked the fact that I skimmed a couple of hundred dollars off what I gave him. Most whores would give up their entire amount, rather than risk an ass beating; but I knew Billy needed me too much, and got too much from me to lay a hand on me. The best part about it - I still couldn't be called a whore. Instead, I was taking "stings" on every corner. Stings were always worth it because they were usually worth two grand, or more. I remember my first sting was for $2800.00. It was a rather simple task, as was everything that came after that. At that point, turning out money became second nature to me.

I didn't feel like I was part of his stable, I felt different. In my mind, I was different, I had taken a skill I learned out of pure survival and applied it to one of the slickest games in the streets, I took the two oldest professions, thievery, and prostitution, and made it work to my advantage. I was pimping the game like no other and Billy was so proud of me; he let everyone know that I was his. I didn't protest, since he always gave me my props and my money's worth. I think Billy knew he had it made with me since I was raking in thousands of dollars every day. Soon, we had enough to get a brand new townhouse, and still keep his old place at the Taj with Sunny. We furnished our townhouse, piece by piece, without a cent of our own cash. His special gift to me was a round, king-size, mushroom-top bed. I remember when he went to purchase the bedroom set; he gave the clerk cash. I watched where the clerk put the money, so I could then go, and steal it right back.

Even though I was good, there was still always room to be better. Eventually, I came across a girl named Black Pat. She was a Boston gal and a mean one at that. To this day, I have never seen anybody top Pat's skills. Most people are said to have a green thumb. Well, Pat had a golden thumb. She was so treacherous with putting her thing down; meaning she never split hers down the middle. As far as she was concerned, all you ever deserved was a tip. She was so good at what she did, that she was the only woman her man had. She was able to take care of both of them well enough. She was all he needed. That bitch could come up with thousands and thousands of dollars every day, all day. No one, not even me, could match her pickpocket game. She never took a dick out or anything. All she needed was two minutes, and it was over; wallet turned, money out, and wallet returned. Nothing but one hundred dollar bill each and every time. I knew that I had to learn that technique. I used to go with her, and most of the time I wouldn't know exactly how much the lick was for. As a result, I had to be satisfied with what we called gapples (GAP). Gapples was basically whatever she felt like giving me. Even though I had a hell of a lot of respect for Pat, I knew this game could not go on with me accepting GAPs. One day, I got fed up, and said to her, "Look… You go your way, and I'm going mine!" She didn't say a word, and let me off on my own. The first couple of times, I wasn't as smooth as I would have liked, but it was just a matter of time before I had it mastered. In exchange for accepting GAP for a short period of time, I was able to soak up the game from Pat which goes to show that the game isn't to be told, but to be sold.

It didn't matter where or who the guy was. He didn't even have to want pussy. All I needed was to be near him for two minutes, and he was hit. Sometimes the lick would happen so fast that I wouldn't have time to put the wallet back. Oddly enough, I still felt inclined to get the wallet back to them somehow. Usually, I shoved it in the nearest mailbox for them to find. After all, I was a thief, not a total bitch. After all, it's honor amongst thieves, right?

Another woman I picked up some good skills was Nikki. Her pimp, Charlie Moon, moved nearby where Billy and I lived, so we met up pretty quick. She was the breaking and entering artist. Her marks were hotels, and she had that game locked tight. She would begin work around 3:00 am, and she would be finished by the time the sun rose. My curiosity peaked and the temptation was itching. I knew I had to try that game too. I wanted to know it all. I began "creeping" with Nikki, and that became our job: "the creepers." While everyone else was sleeping, we would be creeping. During those days, we could use cards to enter the rooms. Sometimes we got lucky, and they might have even "left us" a key. Sometimes, they would have the window open and we simply just had to cut out the screen. Working at night made my vision amazing in the dark. It usually only took a couple of minutes, but the payout was always huge. We would get good jewelry and a whole lot of cash. Sometimes we would take the credit cards, and use them at the all-night boutiques. Most of the time, we would just be satisfied with the cash and jewelry, since I still had a thing about not taking plastic. For the first time in a long time, I almost felt complete. I was a well-rounded hustler - a jack-of-all-trades and a master of them all. My pickpocketing and creeping had people in my "life" making me feel like I was some type of celebrity. My name was ringing bells all over town. I was getting a lot of attention so Billy started getting a little static from the others, even from Sunny - the white girl who was technically his "bottom bitch" who had been with him for years.

Regardless of the amount of attention I was getting and the money that came of it. I was growing tired of the Miami scene and constantly told Billy that I wanted to venture out. Pimps never had a problem venturing out on new territory. Billy had heard about the happenings in Tampa, so we agreed to try it out. Moving up meant Billy would have to keep a closer eye on me. I was just 18 years old and was already in high demand with all of the known pimps. They talked about me as if I was some sort of legend, even though I was only a youngster. Billy knew this better than I did, and where most men might have beaten me to keep me in line, he knew my game well enough, never to raise a hand to me. As long as he took excellent care of me, I was *not* going anywhere. Black Pat's name was ringing also, but since her old man, Maurice, had been killed, she was somewhat paranoid. Even though her skills were highly sought after, she just chilled and decided to go home. I guess she needed time to herself to recoup after losing her man.

Billy sent Cynt and me to Tampa, by ourselves. When I got there, it was like putting a starving kid in a candy store without supervision. Tricks were all over the place; not even the prostitutes stood a chance. By the time, the tricks got to the hotel room or wherever they were going, all the money was already gone. One of the first places we hit up was a club called the Alibi on Dale Mabry. At first, it was cool that we were hanging out there, but the minute the prostitutes realized that they were in a den of thieves; all eyes were on us, especially me. Everyone there was regulars, so of course our new faces stood out like sore thumbs. There were mostly white girls, since the black girls weren't up on the thieving game, and especially not on our level. They were straight-up "flat-backers", meaning all they did was fuck for a buck.

I was clocking so much cheddar in Tampa that I decided to share the wealth and holler at some of my peeps in Miami to come down. We also brought the Ohio Players crew in, I knew the girls since they had just moved in across the street from Billy. We didn't call on the girls in Memphis because they were too damn wild. After all, we were professional whores who only had to look the part. By the time each of the crews got there, we started causing total havoc throughout the town. We were going all over the place -whoring, creeping, and pickpocketing; especially, in St. Petersburg and Clearwater, which was right across the bridge from Tampa. We were cleaning out so well, that most of the local pimps were furious. By now, Billy had gotten comfortable and would only come to Tampa every now and then, but occasionally, I would go to Miami. I liked it that way because I loved being in Tampa. I didn't have to worry about seeing my family, or anyone else that I didn't want to see. Now that I had a new place to run, I decided to take on a new identity. I went by the name of Equilla Jones. I quickly took to my new identity and took pride in the fact that I was high up enough to have my own criminal alias.

Being on my own, and out from under Billy's thumb was causing me to become a little hungry for a new man to play with and as usual, I didn't have to look for too long. One night, while riding by the Alibi, I saw a pimp they called, "Pimp Joe." I was automatically attracted to him; Joe was a lot younger than Billy was, and boy, was he some kind of fine! Girls wanted him, but they didn't know how to get him. I wanted the challenge, so *I* chose him. After he and I met, he would come around, and I could tell from his actions that he was feeling me. As fine as he was, the people that knew him didn't want me to screw myself over and be in for more than I bargained for basically telling me that everything that glittered wasn't gold. They let me know very quickly that Joe had a reputation for getting physical with his women. That didn't scare me though. Even if it was true, I felt like I was more than enough woman to turn him around. I was something brand new to Joe because he didn't have any thieves on his team, just prostitutes. He usually took care of the big cash cons. He used to run the "till" game which meant hitting up the cash register; once the store clerk would open the register, he would switch the bills. He was never one to show any great emotions or any real affection, but I could tell he was happy. After he and I hooked up, I can't remember him staying away from me for one single night.

Eventually, the time came when I had to let Billy know that I had made a decision to be with Joe. I wasn't concerned about Joe being able to handle the situation, he wasn't a punk at all. We went to Miami to give Billy the news - as they called it, "take the pimping to the choosing." I showed Joe where Billy and I lived. When I saw that house, my heart jumped up into my throat, and, for a split second, I felt that I would be leaving behind everything I worked so hard for on one hell of a chance. By then, it was too late to turn back. Once we arrived at the house, Joe got out of the car and went to the door, where Billy immediately met him. Billy had on his robe, where he concealed his gun. Joe didn't realize Billy had the gun on him until it was in his face. Joe had his piece too, but left it in the car with me. I was scared to death and just sat frozen in the car while the scene unfolded. I could hear Joe telling Billy how the game goes and all we came for was my jewelry and clothes. Billy shot one look at me, then back to Joe with a rage in his eyes, as if he wanted to kill him. Thank God, something compelled him to put his gun down. I don't know how, but he must have been expecting us, because he pulled something, what appeared to be my jewelry, out of his robe pocket, and threw it into a wooded area across from the parking lot. We didn't have time for too much trouble, since all the noise caused one of the neighbors to call the police. By the time the police arrived, Billy had hidden the gun. They asked what the problem was. I immediately jumped out of the car and became an actress. I told the police a dramatic story about my boyfriend and I having an altercation and him running through the woods when he heard us coming and basically explained it was because I didn't want to be with him anymore. Much to my surprise, they bought it and left without another word.

A piece of me felt bad for Billy because I knew he had so much faith in me. I just knew that nothing lasts forever and I wanted more. I wanted control, and at that moment I was able to get that from Joe. He still wanted to make it appear as if he wasn't emotionally attached, but in my own little way, I knew better. He always showed me more attention than he did the other women, and in return, I turned his little game into a gold pit. By now, I was terrorizing Tampa. I was hitting up everybody, tricks and all. If it could be removed, it was mine. After the first set of diamonds I took, Joe took me to the dentist and had a ½ carat placed in my teeth, along with another gold tooth. He also had more jewelry customized for me, making the jewelry Billy threw into woods that seemed like pennies in a bucket. Soon after that, I was the baddest, best-dressed, jeweled-out chick in town. I demanded it that way, and that's what I got all the way down to the tailored clothes I had to match Joe's pink El Dorado.

Joe and I became inseparable but he was still slow on showing emotions. A year later, I started to figure out why - Joe was impotent. At first, I was puzzled by how off things were when we had sex he never really got hard. For almost a year, I questioned it but kept it to myself. I guess I didn't really sweat it, because hard or not, he could still make my toes curl and straighten my wig all at the same time. During the time we were together, I became rather domestic and played almost a housewife role I even learned how to prepare certain dishes. My sister, Gail, knew the lifestyle I was living, but I led Momma to believe that Joe was in a singing group. She never trusted that lie even though deep down I'm sure she knew and just didn't discuss it; after all, I had already left home. Sadly, things never stayed perfect for long in my world.

One night when I was creeping into St. Petersburg I found myself in a room where a couple was asleep. I was near the bathroom when the female woke up; because she thought, she heard a noise. She nudged the gentleman, but he didn't move, so she settled back down. I barely took a breath because I didn't want to make a sound. I ended up sitting and waiting under the sink in the dark for almost the entire night. After all that trouble, I was not about to leave there without what I had come for. When I finally made it home, Joe wanted to know where I had been. I tried to explain, but obviously, he thought I had been elsewhere. He and I had a big fight and he ended up splitting my head down to the white meat and breaking my hand. I left him, got treatment at the hospital, and didn't tell the police who was responsible for what happened to me.

I went back to Miami with a split head and a broken hand; and nonetheless, life went on. Blind, crippled, or crazy, I still had to get my hustle on. The cast hindered me from being able to pickpockets, but it didn't do a thing to hold off my itch for money. One day, I wanted to work so badly, that I removed the cast myself and made me a nice lick. My hand was far from being healed, so I had to put the cast back on. I got sick of being sick and tired and had enough of being physically and financially crippled. I wasn't broke but I was a far cry from how I was, so I took the cast off prematurely again, and for good. I had to go back to hustling - there was just no other way for me to live.

CHAPTER 8

It's no profession in the streets that's going to bring you a clean way of living. No matter how easy the lick may look there is always the chance that something is going to go wrong and an even bigger chance of being caught with your hands dirty. I've had so many narrow escapes that I couldn't possibly write about them all, although a few are forever vividly implanted in my memory and carry too many lessons to not be told.

I remember a hustle that a girl and I set up against her trick. She wanted me to come to the hotel, and get the money while she kept her trick busy. Once I got in the room, I had to alter my plans, as I sometimes did. The trick had his leg positioned over by a chair where he had thrown his clothing. I was still determined to get my lick, so I crawled on the floor, removed the clothes, worked the pockets, and rolled out of the room. Just as I was about to get up off my belly and sneak through the half-open door, he made a move for his clothes. Seeing them thrown all over the place, he finally realized what was going on, and looked up just in time to see me halfway out the door. He attempted to come after me, but I was long gone. Getting away wasn't the hard part, but it scared me plenty since I wasn't sure if the guy saw my face or not. I was furious once the girl found me, to collect her half of the money. As far as I was concerned, I had done well on my half of the deal, but she didn't distract him long enough, otherwise he wouldn't have gotten up so quickly. Be that as it may, I didn't try to undercut her share. We had a rule: if it was your trick, and I stole the money, we would split the lick. Then there was my personal rule; what's mine is mine and if you didn't meet me halfway, then what's yours became mine too! I was almost hoping the girl wouldn't find me, since this lick had plenty of cash for me to play around with.

After a couple of weeks, I managed to look past my split head, so I got back with Joe. He needed me too much to try to pull that kind of crap all over again. By the time I got back, he and I had created a strong following. Pimps all over wanted me to teach their girls the art of pickpocketing. The only problem with that was that I felt either you had it, or you didn't. To be great at anything, you have to have a love of the "craft," whether it's hairstyling or hustling. Nevertheless, I did turn out a few girls in the Tampa area, who were packed with "talent." Some girls knew how to strip a wallet like you wouldn't believe. To this day I know of at least one chick who learned from me who's still working her magic. I wasn't just getting popular among the Pimps though - the more girls I turned out, the more my name started streaming through the streets. Eventually, it wasn't too difficult for the police to put a face with my name. After the police figured out who I was, they began to come at me all the time with any accusations and charges they could come up with. I had to start wearing different disguises of all sorts. Once I outsmarted a trick, I would go in, change my disguise, and go back out on the streets for the next victim.

Eventually, all the attention I was causing became too much; and it was time to take our show on the road. Our first stop was New York City, but I didn't know if I was ready for the big city, or not. There were already so many prostitutes, pimps, peep shows, street life, and illegal activities that could entertain people all night and day for those who wanted it. I never experienced that kind of life, at that pace but I welcomed the challenge. We had to make a name for ourselves quickly since New York thieves and pickpocketers were territorial. We had to be careful not to step on the wrong toes, especially for us out-of-towners. I caught on quickly to the way they played their game. I realized that I had to be a bit more aggressive than usual. I started on 11th Ave. Being on that strip was like being in whore heaven. There were so many girls; which meant you actually had to stand out and work hard to get yours. It was a little different from what I was accustomed to, but I managed. There were so many pimps already in New York, that they were all up and down the streets, sporting their mink coats, Caddy's, El dogs, and even a few Mercedes. There were the black pimps that had thieving white whores, and then some of the regular old flat backers. While the pickings were good in New York, it was proving to be a bit too crowded for us. The more saturated and crowded a place was the smaller the share of money there was to be had.

After staying in New York for a short time, we decided it was time to move on to the great city of Boston. When we arrived in Boston, the first thing we did was get lost! Somehow, we ended up in South Boston. Now, back in the 70s, that was the wrong place for black folks to be seen, especially someone in our line of work. After going in circles for almost an hour, we got up the nerve to stop and ask for directions. There were no black folk around to talk to, so we had no choice but to roll up to a white man. The moment Joe rolled down the window to ask the honky for directions, the man threw a hard snowball through the window and hit me dead in my eye. Joe jumped out of the car, but I pleaded with him to get back in so we could leave in one piece without any more injury. This was not our turf and I didn't want any trouble with whites unless I knew I could beat them. Joe seemed to have gotten the idea, so he got back in the car and sped off without another word to me about the incident. We finally got to where we were going. By the time we arrived, I needed a pick-me-up. Since I knew Black Pat was around, I gave her a call to let her know that her girl was in town. She came to where we were staying, and it felt so good to see an old familiar face. She seemed to be doing a lot better since the last time I saw her, and she was even almost back to the old Black Pat I used to know. We got a little info on the city from her like some of the best places to hit a lick and she headed out.

I liked being in Boston because all you had to do was get around the flat backers. As the flat backer approached the cars, I would invite myself up to the car for just one minute and come up with a lick - such as a necklace, watch, or whatever was in reach; jewelry wasn't hard to get. I would look at the lock on the necklace, and then maneuver it around to unsnap it, while all I did was act as though I was being overly friendly or was interested in turning a trick. The men were always so excited since I was all over them, that they never even noticed. It was sweet, just like that. As easy as it was, I still took precautions sometimes. My rule was never to get in the car with a trick. Sometimes that even meant hanging through the window to get at them. Sure, it would hurt a little if they suddenly pulled off, but it would be better than having to worry about him actually bringing me back in one piece. The whores didn't stand a chance against us and were no competition.

There were still places where stealing wasn't as easy as it should have been. Boston's Chinatown was a big challenge, they were some of the most difficult people to "bump" (pickpocket) more than any other place I had ever been. Like always, I relished the challenge, as did Black Pat. It was hard going, but we still managed to make a few licks and a few close calls. One time, in Chinatown, a trick managed to catch me in the act, and had the cops all over my ass in minutes. They were going to charge me for larceny, but I gave the money back, so the cops just sent me on my way. I have a feeling they just kept the money for themselves; even cops had a bit of hustle in them if they knew they could get away with it.

Joe and I finally left Boston and ventured down to Philly. I had never enjoyed "bumping" before as I did while we were in Philly. They had all those one-way streets; all you had to do was cop a red light, and when it turned green, you let them go on their way. They didn't have any other choice since they had to go with the flow of traffic. It was usually the same routine - I would pull the line to reel them in, "We got freaky girls, oriental girls, white or black. Let me give you my phone number so you can give me a call." Then I would ask if they had a pen; as soon as they reached for their pen I made my hit. Sometimes it would be their wallets, or sometimes I might only come away with a nice piece of jewelry. I still remember the phone number I used for so many years. It was whatever the area code was, followed by 777-9311. Most of the time you would say it so fast that they didn't understand it anyway which gave you more time to get stuff. Sometimes, I would come up with the goods, without even putting in much effort. Once they left, I would just go to my next spot and set my trap. I didn't ever want to bump for small change, because those were the worst kickbacks. Men who only had a little money were always the ones to give you problems. They would make you "catch a case" for sure, meaning, getting charged with criminal activity. I don't know why the small stings gave me the most trouble, but I was never caught on the big ones. Now, I see that the logic behind it is those who had money didn't want to be caught up in any situation where it could be revealed that they were trying to buy pussy, or be caught in an area where prostitution was known. It was mostly the married men and professionals who would just take the loss whereas the men with petty money acted as if it was their last.

Philly was always crowded on 13th St. and Locust. Chestnut and Walnut was also a good place to find a trick. We worked those areas along with Broad St. all the way down to 1st and 2nd because you could get away with bumping anyone in those areas. I once remember a news crew that was out filming a story, and all of them were distracted enough for me to get tempted. Normally, I would never bump a "brother," but he was with the crew, so he got it too!

As good as Philly was, after catching a few too many cases, we decided to head back down south to Tampa. As usual, Tampa was sweet as ever and welcomed us with open arms. By now, a few more girls were working in Tampa; most of them were flat backers, though. I also ran into a few I knew from Miami. A lot of girls were working for a pimp named Satchel; I had met Satchel a few years earlier when he was trying to turn my friend's sister over to life. He tried hard to pull her in, but she had too much of a mind to fall for it. I liked Satchel because he didn't speak to me like a hooker, but more like a daughter. Whenever things got bad between Joe and me, Satchel always gave me a place to stay and chill.

I knew all of his girls well: Lorinda, Bebe, Tina, and Betty. All of these women had kids by Satchel, but they all seemed to be cool "wife-in-laws.", or as they call it now "sister wives" I used to hang with Bebe the most; she and I would ride together when we went out to make our licks. I always preferred her company because it was better for me not to drive. If I bumped someone from the car, I would be ready to roll out as soon as I came up. Bebe turned out to be my "Lucky Charm" - every time she and I worked together, we came up with something worthwhile. Especially, if by chance, Smokey Robinson's song, "Cruisin" came across the airwaves. It just seemed like an omen; every time we heard it, we always came up big.

Satchel had other whores as well - whores who had been with him for more than 20 years. Thankfully, I wasn't on that type of time. I always needed, and demanded a certain amount of freedom. I couldn't be with a man that had to split his time up a little over here, and a little over there. They considered me an outlaw, which was what they called us girls without a man. Even though I technically still had Joe, I never felt caught up as other girls did about their pimps.

By this time, I had been arrested a few times, and they were trying anything to throw cases at me. It got annoying after a while. Whenever I went to jail, and the cops didn't have a body to put with a pickpocket case, they tried to give me the case. They would show the "vic" a few mug shots, and of course, they would say it was me, the instant my face popped up. It didn't matter if I had done it or not. This one particular trick from Texas even said I pulled a gun on him - which was a straight-up lie. I never used a gun to steal; he just didn't want his wife to know that he had been in a position to be solicited or an area that was known. Eventually, the State managed to rack up enough "evidence" against me to put me up on trial. The State said that if I were to be found guilty in any other cases they would convict me on consecutive sentences. My lawyer managed to get me a plea bargain for three years and I was sent to Lowell Correctional Prison, which was the only female prison in Florida, at the time.

I was only nineteen and people couldn't believe my age. I didn't look like a kid and the street experience I had certainly didn't match my age. Nobody was going to play me or take advantage of me and I made that very clear as soon as I got there. Holding my own in prison wasn't the hard part, it was letting Momma and Daddy know where I was. They took my incarceration somewhat hard, especially after they found out about my alias. I think they took me having an entirely new name as me trying to disown them and my family. I felt really bad for Momma because she wasn't expecting that from me. Daddy didn't think much better, but he was pretty ignorant as to what I was up to. The first thing out of his mouth was, "What are you doing on elevators trying to pick someone's pocket?" They didn't have a clue as to what their daughter was really into.

When I got to Lowell, I was very rebellious. I didn't want to follow rules of any kind, especially those being issued by the whites in charge. Without a doubt, white folks in authority and I were not going to be getting along. Thankfully, after a few months of being in Lowell, they opened a new prison in Broward County, which was much closer to Miami. They started shipping us there by the busloads; the place was brand new and shit was sweet there. The warden's name was Mr. Sorenson. He was a white guy, one of the only ones whom I had ever trusted, at that point in my life. He had a big heart, but I don't think his heart and mind were in the prison system. While most of the staff would punish you for stupid shit, and send you right down to lockup, he would be much more lenient and would instead write you up even if it was a truly punishable offense. We got anything we wanted under Mr. Sorenson

Soon after I got settled there, Black Pat ended up there, much to my surprise. She had received five years in some cases, from being on the run. While we were there together, we made sure to stand out above all the other girls and I am certain it was because we were the most worldly, and had the most arrogant attitudes. There wasn't much change in how we carried ourselves on the streets when we were in prison together. As usual, I wanted and needed to be a top dog, which allowed me to meet all kinds of interesting people who were doing time for all kinds of crimes, including murder. One woman I met was named Betty Haybor, from Haybor Department Stores – who was there to kill her husband. Another legend I was locked up with was named Annie Ruth Branch. She was an amazing thief who earned the nickname #1. We always had some great stories to share. It turned out, that all of us had a lot in common, especially the fact that we all had pimps and if the woman who came through didn't have a pimp you could assure that it was a man who had something to do with the reason she was in prison. Annie's pimp, as it turned out, was the renowned pimp known all over the world as "The Magic, Don Juan."

Along with hearing wild stories about the streets, you see a lot of wild things happening right behind prison walls. One is the story of one of the officers, Mr. Jenks, who was fucking Terri Moore, a fellow inmate. They actually ended up making a movie about her called, "Love Child." Terri didn't look like Mr. Jenks' type, because she was a hippy, and he was an older, conservative gentleman from New York because he didn't see anyone else but her. Everyone knew that they were messing around because they were always together. When she came up pregnant, it was a long time before any of the staff knew. Once they found out, she refused to tell them who the father was. Eventually, though, they figured it out the next thing we knew, Mr. Jenks was history.

While I was locked up, Billy and I had been back in touch. Just like your first love, your first pimp never goes too far from your mind. It turned out that he still had mad love for me, and wanted me to be a part of his life again. As soon as I figured out that I had him wrapped around my little finger, the wheels started turning in my head, and I saw an opportunity. I feigned a sweet voice, sugary enough that even clever Billy believed I had just as much love for him, as I did from the very start. Little did he know, I was just playing the game. I knew neither Joe nor Billy would want to sign the visiting papers, that were needed to come and visit me, so I had Booker T.'s name approved on my list. I told Joe that he was to be my uncle, and I told him to get some I.D. with the fake name so he could visit. Of course, Joe didn't think to keep a low profile. He rolled up to that jail in two different, brand new cars, a classy Caddy and a white El Dorado that his friend drove. When he came into the visiting room, the women acted as though Michael Jackson or the Pope had arrived. They hooped and hollered, and all but threw their panties at him. He always looked good, but his appearance was beginning to change a little. He was using speed and it was beginning to show. As time went on, it showed more and more, enough to start to turn me off. As always, I didn't want anything to do with a junkie.

Even though I kept up with Joe, I was still talking to Billy. He was in Hawaii, and said, that when he came back to the States, he would visit me. Thinking I was clever, I told him to also use Booker T.'s name when he came to visit. While I thought this was a brilliant idea, it turned out to fuck me over, like nothing else. Billy came up as he promised, and lo and behold, Joe decided to roll his ass up on the same day! As my luck would have it, they met up there together. At first, I had no idea. They called me out for a visit like usual, and while I was expecting Billy, there sat Joe. While he was visiting with me, up came Billy. Unfortunately for them, but lucky for me, the guards caught onto the game pretty quick. Since there were now two men with, supposedly, the same name, they pulled Joe out to see who was who. I was so embarrassed. There the two of them were, once again in confrontation with each other over me. They hadn't seen each other since Billy had pulled the pistol out on Joe, two years ago. This was a big scene, and an even bigger mess for me, because neither one of them was the real Booker T. Hayes. Thank God, the guards were always around because it could have been a whole lot worse. Billy was furious with me. He still had not completely gotten over the fact that I left him for Joe, and now here I was playing these games all over again. What had made it worse was that he had come all the way from Hawaii, just to visit me. He figured out that I had been leading him on as if I would get back to him. No doubt, he left pretty pissed off.

They took Booker's name off my visiting list and I didn't speak with Billy for a long time. Joe was pissed off with me as well, but that really didn't bother me too much, because I had begun to look at him a little differently anyways. This broad that came through began bragging about how she knew my man and was broadcasting how he was out there in the streets shooting up and getting really fucked up to the point that he had become a junkie. This was a bad look for me. I literally wanted to kill her. At that point, I wasn't ready to face the possibility that Joe had become a functioning junkie. It was a good thing that he still kept his appearance together, otherwise, I might not have been so inclined to stick with him.

In the meantime, the guards really started to keep an eye on me, especially after the Booker T. incident. They took Black Pat out of my room and got me a new roommate, Eve Postell; she was only 13 years old when she hit the compound. She was with some other kids who beat up a white man, who later died. Some of the older kids got away with less time, but Eve was sentenced to 99 years. This tripped me out; especially after I really got to know her. It just didn't seem right considering that she was practically a baby. Through our conversations, I could tell she was a wise kid for her age. She reminded me a lot of myself - very misunderstood, but with loads of potential to do just about anything. We hung around so much that they had a rumor that I was messing around with Eve. Of course, that was a lie. I only wanted to be her big sister.

I spent a lot of time in the "hole" while in prison. It didn't matter though, because I couldn't get a visit from Billy, or Joe. My Dad used to come to visit me faithfully, even by himself. Which really touched me -I knew, that even for all his roughness, my Daddy really loved me, but showed it in a way I had never seen before. It was just too bad I had to end up in this position to see it. Even though things were rough, I still had not learned my lesson. The following year, 1979, I was finally going to be released from prison.

Before I left for home, I felt I had one last score to settle with one of the officers. Her name was Ms. Premore, and I'll never forget her. She was of course, white, racist, and had a great dislike for me personally.

As soon as 8:00 a.m. rolled around, the shift would change. I waited patiently for her to relinquish control. The minute I saw her, I pulled my dress up, my panties down, and told her to kiss my ass. Too bad I didn't know that I had a few good days left that they could take. She ended up reporting me, so they made me wait, even though my Mom and sister were there to pick me up, on time. Because of my defiance, we weren't able to leave. Finally, the State told them to let me go. This was the end of my first stint and prison and I wasn't sure how people are supposed to feel when they left; refreshed, renewed, and maybe... even thankful. Not me - I was flat-out pissed! I didn't have any warm, fuzzy feelings about anything only bitterness, and anger for what I had been through, those past 3 years. Although, I knew what would make me feel better – to go out and hit a lick. So there I was again, barely out of prison and off to my same scandalous games.

CHAPTER 9

Momma and I went out to eat at Red Lobster before we finally made it home. I can't remember the first person I contacted after getting out of prison. What I do know is that I went to the store and stole some new outfits and shoes. By dark, I was back in stride again. Just as soon as I was out of the store I was looking for a site for my next lick. I was over by the airport where the pilots and airport personnel parked their vehicles. There were also hotels and the Doral Country Club in that area. It was the perfect spot. I collected over a thousand dollars that night. The next day, I went to an old friend of mine and asked her to rent a car for me. The fact that I didn't have a license didn't make a damned bit of difference to me. Soon, I was cruising around in a sweet, rented Lincoln as usual. Not only did it feel good to have my freedom and be back in the streets, it felt good to show off. After just a short period of time, I had come up with a good amount of jewelry and money. Even though I had made enough money to buy my own car quickly, it made more sense to keep renting cars instead. I had other people renting for me because I didn't have a license. I always found the right people to do it who didn't care because they knew I was coming back with cash.

Now that I had wheels again, I was ready to handle my business. I went through all the old neighborhood spots just to let folks know, "The top bitch is back in town, and on a mission to come up." On my welcome home tour, I cruised through Perrine and just so happened to run into

Charlotte and Shirley. This time, being a little more mature and with some out-of-town experience, I felt different being around down south broads. I felt my life had surpassed that dirty-south style. Sure, I wasn't too far above them considering that I was hanging out with hookers, but driving around in a Caddy, wearing long wigs, and hanging out with different women with different tastes for so long made me feel out of place with Charlotte and Shirley. Somehow, in their drunken stupor, they managed to spot me, so I said, spoke and we chatted for a little while. Charlotte was always happy to see me, of course, even though she knew I had been in prison. Still, I didn't feel I had a reason to stick around them for too long, so I didn't.

It turned out that many of the people I knew weren't as I remembered them anymore. I found out where Joe was, and wanted to check him out, but what I found wasn't a pretty sight. He had changed from a pretty boy to a straight-up junkie, like some shit I never seen before. He was always itching, gangly as hell, and had a bad case of the shakes. Seeing him like that made me feel sick since I still didn't want anything to do with junkies. Despite that, I still cared about him, not enough to stick around, but I still cared. We visited for a little while, and then I told him that I would be right back, left, and I knew that I wasn't coming back, not to "Joe the junkie," anyways. Only when he went back home to get himself together, did I start speaking to him again. Besides, I knew that I would miss Fat (Royal); who was Joe's daughter, I adored that little girl and she always admired me, and thought of me as her mom.

In the meantime, I was still all over Miami which was like fresh money. I got paid and didn't have to share with anybody. I still needed a partner sometimes, though. I ended up meeting a Jamaican chick, who was a straight flat backer, and we started riding the strips. She was very familiar with the area so I let her do the driving. We were bobbing, and weaving in and out of hotel parking lots. It was easy to catch the tricks going in, or coming out, and they always had something to take. I was unsnapping all kinds of jewelry. I even came up with my first Rolex watch. At first, I was trying to sell it to one of the drug dealers, he didn't want it but told me that I could probably dump it real quick in Overtown. From my previous experiences with Overtown, knowing the types that hung on that side made me leery about making that move, there was too much of a risk of being cheated, robbed, or worse - being turned in, and I did *not* intend to land my ass back in jail so soon. I avoided Overtown and kept the watch for the time being.

After running it on my own for a little while, I wanted a more familiar partner. So for the first time in a long time, I got in touch with Stocking. Stocking and I worked up and down the highway. I was driving for him and his friends in a car full of guns and drugs. We were in Boston and Pennsylvania, mostly just selling drugs and coming up. For a few months, we stayed in Pennsylvania before we went back to Miami. Being out on the road with Stocking was always a guaranteed adventure. I remember once, we were at this exclusive hotel in Boston; everyone thought Stocking was the sweet-singing Teddy Pendergrass (incognito.) We ended up running up a high hotel bill and ducked out without paying.

Shortly after that, Stocking went to jail for six years. After all, everyone eventually had to pay the piper and it was finally Stocking's turn.I bolted after Stocking went away and was once again left without a good partner not to mention a man. Thankfully, Joe had finally gotten himself together, so we tried to give it another go. He came to Miami, and we moved to Biscayne Blvd, but things quickly made a turn to something more familiar. Within no time, we were right back in Tampa and came up big. I was working twice as hard because I wanted a new car. Within a few months, I had "earned" $30,000, and I was ready to purchase my two-toned, champagne and brown, Cadillac Seville. Finally, we were starting to rise back to the top of the chain in style. I was getting so much jewelry that we had bags and bags of it just lying around our apartment, waiting for someone to hock. We kept some of it while others we had melted down and made into some specially designed unique pieces.

Joe and I were still hitting it big, one night we were on Dale Mabry and I came up with a piece of jewelry that was worth about $40,000. At first, I almost didn't want to tell Joe how much the piece was worth but then again, I never let him know exactly how much money, or jewelry I was working with. We decided to take the piece to this diamond exchange on 163rd St & NW, in Miami. We went in both looking up to par, not like a couple of poor folks that you would expect to rob a joint. People thought we were some sort of entertainers or something. We went to have the piece appraised and as soon as the jewelers saw it we had their undivided attention. The sales lady was very eager to assist me, in whatever I needed. Little did she know, I was about to come up out of there with whatever I desired, whether I paid for it or not. She came out with this exquisite solitaire piece. She said it was valued at around $10,000 and said that it was "Something that a lady should never take off." So, I took her advice! I got Joe's attention, showed him the necklace, and gave him the sign that I was leaving with what was on my neck. I got so excited that I left Joe standing right there. Later on, he and I met back up at the hotel. He told me that he had to act as if he had given me a ride, so the woman didn't think that he knew me. He was a little pissed that I ditched him, but he came up with a pouch full of jewelry too which kept me out of trouble.

All of this took place in 1980, the same year as the Mariel BoatLift. A well-known time when a large number of Cuban refugees came to Miami. During this time it was easy for me to come up with drugs, as well as cash because it was everywhere and always in whatever pockets I was hitting, especially over on 8th Street - that's where all the big, Cuban drug dealers were located. I couldn't speak a word of Spanish, but I was over on their side of town cleaning them out almost every other day. It got to the point where I had so much jewelry, that I would just leave the money. The jewelry was so much more tempting, and a lot easier to get a hold of, too; especially if I could just slide off with something nice, like a Piaget. Hanging around the Cubans proved to be more dangerous than robbing plain white folk, though. One time, I remember stealing money from the "wrong" Cuban. As soon as I made the hit he caught me and asked for a kickback. The lick was too good, and I wasn't about to give him anything back, but he left and came back with a gun... so, I ran for my life. Thankfully, there was a girl I knew, who was staying at the hotel I was at, so I immediately ran to her room. I could hear him firing up a storm behind me, but I didn't dare to look back. After that close call, I caught a couple more cases, but most of the victims didn't come back to town. Because of that, either the charges got dropped, or I pleaded out.

After that mess, Joe and I went back to our safe-haven spot once again, in good old Tampa. He ran into some people he knew who had the "check game" on lock – this was a con that Joe mastered over time. He recruited some of his workers to run up into banks and steal the garbage including blue photocopies of customer transactions. From there, we handed the info over to Alpo, who could forge just about anything and anyone's handwriting. Even with the "payroll" we had to shell out to Alpo and the rest, we still made a lot of money. Joe kept his hands full in the con because he was clocking thousands, and thousands of dollars, every day.

Even though Joe and I were raking in the cash, on the down low Joe had started using again. He tried to convince me that he wasn't. At first, I believed him, or maybe I wanted to believe him since I didn't want to have to walk out again. Eventually, I caught him red-handed - high as a kite. He was so tripped out that he backed me into a corner and demanded I get high with him. I did it, but as always, it wasn't my cup of tea, and now I was pissed. Still, it was a bittersweet finding, since it meant for sure, that I had to walk out on him for good. It would be especially hard this time, after all that we had managed to rebuild. It got a whole lot worse though. While all of this was going on; I found out that the FBI had Joe under investigation. They had been taking photos of us, and our apartment. They were taking pictures of everyone who was coming and going from our spot, which thankfully wasn't too many people. Even though the FBI was on to us, we continued doing our thing - FBI or not, we still had to eat.

One of Joe's recruits got busted and the feds started looking for Joe. We spotted the surveillance team trailing us, so we got the hell out of dodge and headed down to stay in Missouri with one of his daughters. Even though we were careful since we knew that they were on to him, the police still managed to corner him and lock him up. Joe got hit harder than any of us had expected; he received an organized crime charge, otherwise known as a RICO. Since I was involved, I expected to land myself right back in jail, still after everything, I put him through; Joe came through for me. He took the heat for the whole rap, just to make sure I would stay out of jail.

Since there was nothing left for me in Tampa, I returned to Miami and held up as best as I could. Even there, everyone was coming at me, including younger girls who were trying to get on the bandwagon. They wanted to know how I was getting my ends, and they wanted to learn the art of it, too. I took a few of them under my wing, and some even turned out to be decent thieves. Meanwhile, I was staying with my sister, Gail, until I could lease another apartment. Even back at home, I couldn't keep myself out of trouble. I ended up back in trouble with the law, because of a guy who worked the dumpsters; he came across over $100,000.00 in blank traveler's checks. I started working the traveler's checks for a long while, until, like an idiot; I went into the American Express office. They immediately turned me in to the authorities, and, because I was on probation, held me. I went through a program at first, but I had to go back to Tampa for charges, that I hadn't yet been to court for. It looked like jail all over again for, I was praying that I would get lucky and miss taking another trip to prison and as it turned out, I still had a little luck on my side. I narrowly escaped that scene, leaving Tampa once again, and began to look for work elsewhere.

CHAPTER 10

As eager as I was to see Stocking again, I was still thinking about Joe. Part of me knew he was turning into a no-good junkie, but the other part of me still wanted him. With this in mind, I went up to Missouri to try to give our relationship another shot. He and I had been back and forth to Miami, picking up cocaine - nothing big, usually no more than a kilo at a time. I preferred to drive because I was better than most men were at handling stressful situations. Things stayed good for a little while, we were making some decent hits, and Joe seemed to keep it together well enough. However, after one of the trips we were in Joe's uncle's house, and I caught him shooting up. He knew that would make me leave in a heartbeat, but obviously, he didn't care. I had given him enough chances; it was time to leave for good. The only real regret I had, was leaving Joe's daughter, Royal Tijuana, because she was the closest I'd ever come to having a kid of my own but, it didn't matter, I had to look out for myself and I had to leave, it was final.

I hollered at a friend of Joe's, named Touché. At first, I didn't expect much, after all, Joe was his boy but Touché ended up coming through for me all the same. Turned out, that he had a crush on me, which I quickly used to my advantage to get what I wanted. We plotted my departure right under Joe's nose. He took me to Memphis to fly out to Vegas where my old friend Gerry was living. She and I didn't waste a second going right to work on the strip clocking every lick possible. Black Pat had since gotten out of jail, too and she joined us out in Atlantic City. We had a regular hustling trio which quickly became a foursome when a girl I met a year earlier named Brandy wanted to join. She came in wanting to learn and to move just like me and I must say she could come damn close sometimes. Little as she was, she was just as fast as Pat and I were. Gerry on the other hand had her own way of doing things, as she was very subtle and patient, but she was good too.

Vegas wasn't as big as it is now back in the 80's. It consisted of the famous Las Vegas strip, most of which is now considered "old Las Vegas" and the West Side, where all the black folk hung out. My girls and I thought it best to hang on that end, that way it was less suspicious and we knew we could make a killing selling all the shit we stole from the boutiques. I could sell a high-end outfit like Lily Rubin which at that time could go for almost 15,000 dollars a pop. But I rarely kept real expensive stuff, Gerry did. She loved to flaunt herself like she was Patty Labelle; she dressed to impress at any party, even though she'd be stealing right out of a man's back pocket while they were busy keeping their eyes right on her.

Vegas was always known as a party city and my girls and I used that to our advantage. Usually, at parties, we would come up on men and their wives, while acting drunk out of our minds. We'd fall all over both of them and come away with cash and jewelry every time. Usually, the couple were too smashed to even notice that anything of theirs had gone missing until it was too late. I liked to party myself and after a good round of Hennessey, you could bet on me acting crazy. Once, my girls and I were up at a liquor store at a convention center and I came up on a trick after some heavy drinking. From what I could tell he didn't look like he had a whole lot of money, but in Vegas you could never really tell who was loaded and who wasn't. Turned out he had a fat roll stuffed in his pocket, and I was too drunk to even pretend I wasn't trying to steal.

He tried to push me away, but even as drunk as I was, I tore his ass up for that money. We must have fought for a good ten minutes before my girls called me away. I did get some money, but not the whole amount he had and not enough to say that the whole incident was really worth it and that was the thing, in hindsight, many of my experiences and quick come-ups were worth the trouble I'd encounter in the end, only the money and the thrill of the at the moment.

It didn't matter how much experience I had at that point- I still got into trouble. One day I was in front of the MGM Grand scoping out potential tricks. I spotted one, walked up beside him, as if I was going into the Casino, and then made conversation. I mentioned something about a party which, of course, was a bunch of bullshit but I kept on making up more things to talk about and details of the party until I got the stash. I was trying to be as cool as I could, so I didn't make him leery before we reached the entrance. Too bad, he had enough sense to touch his pocket and quickly realized his roll was gone. He gave me a hard look, and said in his thick Texan accent, 'Give me that fucking roll bitch." If I had somewhere to run, I would have but it was broad daylight, and I didn't want to make a scene. I was in a no-win situation, because my car was parked too far away, and traffic was too packed for me to call a cab so in this particular situation I had to kick it back. I was mad after I looked at the stash; it had to be a good twenty thousand of brand-new money with the wrapper still on and everything. Normally, I would have never kicked back in a situation like this but I didn't want to end up in jail or the morgue because for that kind of money, he would have been ready to kill my ass and looked like he would.

The tricks in Vegas were damn clever. The city is full of schemes, scams, addictions, and people looking to come up. Just as we were addicted to the thrill and money that comes with robbing, most of the tricks were addicted to gambling, pussy, or something that put them in a mindset of always trying to outsmart someone. Whether it was the table dealers, drug dealers, or the hoes, they had a slick way about them, too, which presented a challenge at times. Brandy and I were in front of Caesar's Palace when we ran up on this trick. Brandy bumped him and then went to pass me the wallet back. I put it in the opposite pocket and we kept going. We kept our eyes on him, just to make sure he wasn't a kickback. It soon proved to not even be worth it, because his money was low; he had less than $500 in his wallet. As I said before, it was always the chump change that got you fucked up. We saw the trick feeling his back pockets, and he knew something was wrong. His wallet was in the wrong pocket! By now, we were trying to get out of sight without causing a scene. We weren't fast enough, though, and ended up getting busted. I dealt with the cops easily but was slammed with another larceny charge.

For many years it didn't matter how many times I was arrested or caught. To me this was my livelihood and how I ate so as soon as I got away with it or didn't catch many wrecks from the authorities it was back to work and business as usual. After Vegas though I felt like it was time to step my game up. It wasn't that I was getting small money, but picking pockets on the street wasn't enough of a challenge anymore. Not only that, there seemed to be no end game in it, and doing the same thing in the streets of Vegas was daunting. I decided that it was time to step up to swiping credit cards. Since money and spending money flow like water in Vegas, it was easy to get away with swiping and they were loose on checking your card. Anything went on the Vegas strip. Just whip out a traveler's check, sign a somewhat close signature, and you were made. We ran the game twenty-four-seven. Most clerks turned a blind eye, even if they knew you weren't being straight with them, especially if they made a commission. I could have fine jewelry and furniture shipped right to me. As long as the card took, it was a done deal and it didn't matter if the address matched the card or not; it all depended on how good your card was. The best place to find good cards with high limits was where people intended to spend big money. My crew and I would head to an Open House, and while the owners thought we were looking to buy, we were busy picking their pockets clean of cash and credit. By the time they left the house or realized their cards were gone, they had already been swiped.

I played that scheme for a while and took to traveling on airplanes, with all the cash I was pulling in. Even there, I found plenty of opportunities to work my fingers. You'd be surprised how much you can pick off a bag in an overhead bin when no one is smart enough to watch you. People who left their stuff under the seats were even easier to grab. All I had to do was reach under, flip open a bag, wallet out, cash out, and back before they even knew they'd been hit. I was smart this time, though; I never stripped a wallet clean. Usually, I would grab a card or two, and always leave the little money. That way if they took a quick glance into their wallet, they would see the green I left and would assume the rest was there without bothering to count.

My crew and I started making a statement on the West Side of Las Vegas. Even the Pimps knew they couldn't touch us. No man, black or white, could tell me to do shit. Everyone knew what we stood for: independence. If we wanted a man, we took him, not the other way around. We were renegades, and it was a privilege for one of the pimps to even get a glance. We'd go to any club we'd like: The Moulin Rouge, West Side Story, anywhere and everywhere, until just the look on our faces made the men drop the rope, and let us through. On the west side, your "piece" spoke louder than you did, and my girls and I had gotten into enough shootouts to earn a good deal of respect. Although it didn't matter how good we got, people still tried to play my girls and me. I met up with a fellow thief, named Rita; who although wasn't up to my level was cool, for a little while anyway. I figured out Rita wanted to befriend me for her own benefit, which became crystal-clear, once she introduced me to her man, Cato. She thought she could play me, but she didn't know who she was messing with. She tried to win me over by showing the nice cars her man gave her and bragging about how good he was to his women. I liked my freedom, though, and as far as I was concerned, Joe was the last Pimp I'd ever be with. I bit, but in reality, I knew I had to play the bait to my own advantage.

I kept Cato in my corner long enough, so that if I went to jail, he would get me out, but he wasn't good for anything else. Even after Rita, people were still dumb enough to try to challenge us. They'd mess with us, just to get a name for themselves, but it never did much for them. Whenever any little Vegas girl would try to get slick with me, Brandy and I would always shrink them down back to size and shove them back into place. We also had a couple guys try it with us, but that only ended in me shooting up their cars while Brandy drove quickly sending the message to back off and that we were not the ones to play with. These guys were supposed to have had a name out there but were no comparison to what we had going on. But alas, my work in Vegas soon caught up to me and I began stacking on charges, I decided that I needed to step up my game elsewhere, so I flew back to Miami.

CHAPTER 11

Before heading down to Miami, I got in contact with a friend of mine who they called "Flowerman." He and I knew we could make a killing on the West Side selling drugs, so we discussed plans to head down there and work together. Gerry and I, as well as Brandy's boyfriend, Carlos, made formal plans. I had a feeling that the entire time, they were skeptical about me really getting into selling drugs. But, hell, we had done everything else, so I didn't see any harm in making life easier and stepping onto a new playing field. I went to Miami the very next day. Flowerman picked me up from the airport, and we spoke briefly about what he expected, and what I should (and should not) do - about selling drugs. I was listening, but most of it was common sense. He said, "Never let customers know that it's your shit; always say that it belongs to somebody else. Also, if they take the drugs don't let them bring them back to you." He went on and on until I stopped listening altogether, but I let him talk, lest I wound his manhood.

After we had gotten comfortable, we had a few drinks, tooted some powder, and started to relax. I was waiting to see what he was like in bed when, suddenly, he received a phone call, and upon ending the call, he said he had to make a run. At that time, people were coming down from Cali to trade cocaine for heroin. Had I been on the phone I would have known that he was getting played. Somebody had other ideas of what was going down, but Flowerman wasn't as alert then and clearly wasn't taking his own advice. He got there, thinking he was going to make a routine trade, but they jumped him on the spot. They robbed him and beat him so badly, that they bent the barrel of the gun over his skull. They would have shot him too, but they bent up the gun so badly that it could not fire. Flowerman had enough sense in him to hold his breath and play dead long enough for the Cuban thugs to stop beating him. We found him a few hours later, left for dead, and barely breathing. After seeing what had happened to Flowerman, I started having second thoughts about the whole drug-running idea. There he was, telling me who, and what not to trust, only to be robbed the same night. After I found out just how easily they had tricked him and jumped him, it made me have second thoughts about what I wanted to do with him.

I really wasn't too keen on dealing, but decided to linger around Miami for a bit longer, while Flowerman was in the hospital, recuperating from his broken ribs and concussion. Besides, he needed someone to keep his business running smoothly; even half-dead, he was hard to play and kept his hustle about him. When he gave you a kilo, and said the price was $25,000, that was what he expected back - and not a dime less. It was on me to break it down, like a double barrel; I had to get mine so I stepped on it so that I could double my money. That meant that for me to make money, I cut raw dope so that I was able to process not one, but two kilos, sell both, then take the profit from the second one. Other times I could just double the price; I was selling good shit, so people didn't even question how much I charged, especially out in Detroit. After a sale, I usually gave Flowerman his cut-off top; I kept up the routine until he could move around on his own again. Once he got home, he sent me out on the road with a trunk full of powder. He sent Howard with me as my "Cap-man," which put him in charge of keeping me out of trouble, and he turned out to be a pretty decent guy.

We stopped in Philly first. Since I had some contacts there, I squatted until I got rid of my packages. I still wanted to keep some for later, so I broke them down into quarters and went to the streets. Philly went for it, and I got paid big! Next, we flew out to Detroit. During the flight, I met a guy who immediately showed a lot of interest in me. He tried to holler at me, and it turned out he had a suspicion about the type of person I was and I felt the same way about him. Some things you just know. He hinted that he was in the game, and tried to drag me into saying more than I needed. During this period, you didn't have to worry too much about snitches, but I figured it wouldn't hurt to play it safe. At first, I didn't talk to him too much, but it was enough for me to feel comfortable that he was trustworthy enough. We arranged to meet up once the plane landed, so we could trade information. I still knew better than to trust him completely, though. In any case, I needed to catch him off guard and get there with my shit without giving him time to plot on me. When we finally met up, both of us dropped the friendly passenger act, and got down to business. See, I had to let him fear me as much as I feared him because when you're in someone else's territory, the game is even more dangerous. You had to have your piece with you, or else you would be worthless. I put on quite a show and acted just like Flowerman taught me. I made him think I had an army of Columbians with me just waiting on my command if things didn't go according to plan. The boguard, or acting tougher than I really was, definitely came in handy at those times.

I made such a killing, that by the time I got back, Flowerman wanted me to get him a brand new Benz, and pay cash for it. From there, I only got better; I learned to look fear in the eye to the point where I wasn't scared of Flowerman anymore. Like every man I've ever been under, he wanted to show me off to his boys. They knew that I had been stacking that paper for him, and he liked to flaunt it. He would tell me to come down on 22nd Street in Overtown just so they could see him get the sack of money that I had for him. I made him ten times what he had before he started working with me. Soon, he had a Rolex and fly mink coat to show off, which he wore in Miami no matter what the weather was. I continued to take care of my business and made my doubles on it. Flowerman thought he was taking advantage of me, but little did he know that we were taking advantage of each other! Sure, I was taking a risk by playing a dealer, but that was something that came with the game.

I finally contacted Gerry and let her know that I was on my way back to Vegas to sell some dope. She immediately knew what time it was, and she replied, "As soon as you get here, it's gone!" As expected, the dope didn't last long in my hands. At that time I was taking the drugs myself, rather than Flowerman, and sometimes, Gerry would travel with me. I would carry drugs on most trips, but that wouldn't stop me from knocking off the stewardesses. Right off the plane, I went to work. The nearest jewelry store and the most expensive boutique got hit up; even if I couldn't wear the shit, it was mine. There was never a question of whether or not I had money when I walked into a store. I knew how to present myself as anything but the shady thieving nigger that most white folk thought of blacks as.

I made some financial investments during my stints. After all, I needed to have something to show for what I was doing; it was never anything too big or flashy, besides my car and condo in Vegas. I also had to use common sense with my spending because Gerry always lived on the edge, and didn't give a damn about people being suspicious of her lifestyle. She needed two maids because her joint was so big, and even that wasn't enough for her – she just had to have a million-dollar home. Without kids, I saw no need for a big flashy home, besides that, I was a little paranoid about attracting too much attention. Gerry and her boyfriend ignored my paranoia and kept on getting paid for their various schemes.

Flowerman decided to pay me a visit to Vegas. On the way he meant to make a stop in Alabama, but he quickly dropped the plan because he said he felt like was being followed. I knew he had to have eaten some powder; he didn't want anyone to know he ate it or even touched it for that matter, but at that point, it was pretty obvious the way he was tripping over every little thing. I was supposed to pick him up at the airport in Vegas, but he was off a little with the time, so I was late getting there to pick him up. As a result, he blamed me and said he ended up losing about $250,000 dollars, which was in a suitcase in baggage claim. Even though it wasn't my fault that he was too scared to pick it up from baggage claim, it didn't keep him from getting pissed at me. I had just finished ordering a suite for him at Caesar's Palace, when I saw him coming right at me, with steam all but shooing out his ears. I tried to be soft about breaking the ice because he looked crazy with his hair standing straight on his head. It stood so stiff that it looked like horns! He told me what he lost, then demanded $60,000 as payback. I didn't want to cause any more trouble, so I went into my stash so that he could go and gamble. He ended up losing all of it and asked for more. Normally I would never just shell out my money like that, but the whole incident put a lot of pressure on me. After a few days of winning, he decided to leave. I was so happy to see him leave. It was then that I realized how crazy he really was. My emotions for him started to change to the point where it was strictly business between us. The last straw was when I found out, that his old ass was a pedophile. It was found out that he had been having sex with girls as young as 14. The thought was sickening; it reminded me of those dirty old men who infiltrated my life at an early age. As small as his dick was, he needed that to boost his little-dick ego, and could never handle an experienced woman.

Even though I hated him as a person, he had the power that I needed to keep clocking my dollars. Everything else was going great in Vegas, so Gerry and I started looking to expand. I found out that prices were banging down in Memphis, so I decided to move in on it. Gerry and I went to work, and we did that for a while until one of our runs went sour and I turned up short. Gerry and Carlos tried to say that the dope got wet, but I knew that the way it was being packaged wouldn't cause it to dissolve just like that. Anyone who knew the game was fully aware that you didn't throw away wet dope; you either dry it or cook it. I don't know who took it from Gerry, all I cared about was having to deal with Flowerman. The last thing I wanted was to end up owing this crazy motherfucker. I couldn't even imagine what to do or say. Gerry flew down to Miami to get more dope and said it was under the house, but I didn't understand Zip when it came to this business. I wanted to strangle her within an inch of her life, but instead, I sent her back to Miami. I figured that she was the one who fucked up, so she would be the one who dealt with Flowerman. She copped, but somehow I was still short, so I decided I couldn't take the pressure, and flew the coop on his ass.

Thankfully, the only thing Flowerman knew about Vegas was the strip, and he didn't have a clue where to look for me on the Westside. Even though Gerry and I had not spoken since the bad dope deal, I kept on pushing it, since I had made enough contacts on the Westside to continue selling drugs. I had other connections to protect me, so it was no biggie.

I started dating a guy named "Stretch" from the Westside. It was perfect for me since he knew people I didn't. Stretch was a former basketball player for a non-pro league. He made it for a while, but he couldn't keep away from the drugs. I don't know how he did it, but before the games, he would smoke up an eight ball, which is 3.5 grams of coke, and still have enough sense in him to go play ball.

By now, I had stepped my game up and got myself a Condo at Copal Cabana, a nice hideaway off of Boulder Highway. Gerry lived there a little while before me, but thankfully, I never ran into her. I still wasn't fucking with her for fucking things up for me in Miami, because whenever I went back I went with the thought of having to duck Flowerman in the back of my mind. Besides the issues with Gerry, things settled enough for me to invite my parents out to see me. They came separately because by this time they were no longer together. My dad pissed me off when he flew in to visit. He took advantage and decided to go see his sister up in LA. One day, I all of a sudden looked up to realize that he had taken my car to LA and then had the nerve to come back to Vegas with his sister, and another woman. Only God knows who that heifer was; my pops thought he was so slick. He took them back the following day, and I was glad to see them go.

When my mom came to visit, I couldn't keep her away from the casinos. One night, I took her to the grocery store and dropped her there so that she could shop. Several hours went by and she still wasn't back. I began to worry and decided to walk across the street to check out what was going on with her. Before I even got close to the store, I saw my Momma, grocery buggy and all feeding a slot machine! I had to shake my head and laugh because I loved seeing her having such a stress-free, good time. After all she had been through she deserved it, and I was happy to be the one to give it to her. One night, she even went to the Landmark Casino at the Convention Center and won a couple of thousand dollars. She was ecstatic about that. Unfortunately, she began to get homesick and decided the next day that she was ready to leave.

After Mom left, I ended up keeping her rental car for a bit longer. It didn't take long for the gears to start turning in my head. I still wanted revenge on Gerry; for me, it wasn't over. I seriously thought about running her over and probably would have, if I could have found her.

Luckily, I wasn't feeling murderous the night I finally did run into her. I saw her in front of Circus Circus, getting ready to beat a trick. I ran my car right into hers, backed up, and rammed it again. She had a friend of ours, Ruby, in the car with her, but I was mad and didn't even care. I rammed that car until it couldn't move anymore. By now, people were gathering around, so I jumped out, ran toward the Convention Center Street, and caught a cab home. I knew I had just started a war, and even though I didn't know just how it was gonna go, I was ready. At this point, I didn't hate Gerry; we were caught up in the game, and both of us had a point to prove.

Gerry and a few other people knew that I had come across some stolen furniture, and kept a few pieces for my house. Only a few weeks later, I got a knock on my door. When they announced that they were the police, I knew I was fucked. Since there was no way of getting around them I went and got what little drugs I had left, and put them on my body.

Of course, they took me to jail. They didn't say a thing about the drugs. They seemed more concerned about the furniture. Evidently, that was really all they came for. Whoever called must have been smart enough not to mention the drugs, because it would have incriminated them, that's how I came to realize who it was. When they came for me, Stretch wasn't at home, so by the time I was able to make phone calls, I had been placed in a holding cell -thank God the phones were in the cells. I was finally able to get a hold of him, and as I explained to him what was going on, he figured out that I had the stuff still stashed on me. I didn't know if I should flush it, or hold on to it. Then unexpectedly, a girl said that she knew Stretch; I asked him if he knew her, and he said yes. She was on her way out of jail, so I asked her to take the half-kilo to him.

Just as I was being booked, and preparing to make bond, I heard someone say, "She has a hold from Florida." The only person who knew that was Gerry. I thought, "Damn, I'm fucked, and they did get me again." As a result, I had to wait thirty days for Dade County to extradite me. As my luck would have it, they came on the 30th day. Just as they pulled me into the courtroom to explain that they couldn't hold me any longer, the cops showed up to get me, right at the last second. The officers who picked me up thanked me for the free trip to Vegas. They were almost too late in picking me up because they had been up all night. As we were leaving, I started to give them the wrong directions, but since they were being so nice to me, I decided not to fuck around, for once. All it would do was waste time anyway. I was on a one-way ticket back to Miami with a floater from Vegas. That meant that I could never return or I would be subjected to re-arrest.

CHAPTER 12

On my way back to Miami, Flowerman popped up in my mind of course. It was mostly just curiosity; I certainly wasn't worried about seeing him on this trip. As far as I was concerned, I didn't need him for a damn thing anymore - I was a certified drug dealer. Just because I didn't need him though, didn't mean I was very keen on running into him. As long as I owed that man a dollar, he wanted it. Since I was caught up in that police car, and on my way to jail, that meant my regular means of income were completely useless - I was about to be out of commission for a while. My friend, Joyce, did her best to take over the payments at my Condo while she stayed there with my Godson. Even though she tried her damnedest, she couldn't keep up with the payments. Stretch didn't fare much better, since he ended up putting out more than he ever brought in. He finally ended up giving his mom some of the furniture the police left behind.

Williemae Hollingsworth was a lady I had adopted as my Godmother, and she was in charge of a drug program called, "Adapt." She convinced the judge, Ellen Morphoneus, that this program could be very beneficial for me. Ms. Morphoneus was the meanest judge who had ever existed in Florida, and she was rather skeptical when she first saw me because I certainly didn't appear to be the person reflected in my record. She said, that I reminded her of a schoolteacher or a good Samaritan. She even referred to me as a, "distinguished looking young lady"; nothing like what my record showed. I used this to my advantage and worked the courtroom in other ways, as well. When I made my court appearances, I would always wear purple. I found out that purple was the judge's favorite color, and she had a great love for it. Every time I went before her, I made sure I was decked out in purple. It ended up working perfectly, and she was very lenient with me. She approved the idea of me attending the Adapt program. However, I still had the pending charges in Tampa that I had to deal with.

My "rabbit's foot" was working that day and I was to be released from jail. Someone made a mistake while processing me and overlooked my detainer in Tampa. When I found out that I was about to be released, I was surprised but very happy. I went straight home, and that night I called Ms. Hollingsworth to tell her what had happened. She didn't share my optimism, since things like this, according to her, always had a way of turning around, and biting you in the ass. She said that we should wait, and see what happens. Turns out, she was right about not getting excited. The next day I was at my mom's house and the phone rang. I answered the phone, not even considering that it could be the jail, but it was. When they asked who I was, I confirmed the obvious, and they proceeded to tell me about a mistake that they made. I told them to hold on for a minute. I placed the phone down, jumped in the car, and went to take care of everything I needed to. Such tasks included getting some weed to take back to jail, and items I knew I wouldn't be able to get in without sneaking them in. I was not about to go back to jail empty-handed.

I turned myself in after a couple of days. The authorities contacted Tampa, and they came to pick me up. The wonderful part about it was that they ended up running my sentence concurrent with the time I had received in Miami. So once again, I was free. When I was released under one stipulation and that was that I had to go to the halfway house for the Adapt program. We had different meetings daily. I occasionally listened during the meeting, but usually, my mind was focused on more important things - where I would find my next lick. One day, I said I was going "to look for a job." Really, I was looking for my next come-up. Instead, I went down to Richmond Heights. On my way back, I met a Jamaican guy, named Livingston, at the metro rail station, and he kept trying to talk to me. I ended up taking his number because I'll admit - I was interested in seeing what he was about. It didn't matter how he looked, I just wanted to know what he could do for me. I explained my situation to him and asked him if he thought he could help me. He didn't have a problem with it; the only catch was that he was a married man, but that didn't stop me. Little did he know, I would be the one playing him. The first thing Livingston did was rent a car for me. Around the same time, I ran into one of Stocking's friends; he told me where Stocking was, and said that he also wanted to contact me. Stocking was still in prison, but we made contact and started talking again. Even with that going on, Livingston and I were still chatting. Since he was a police officer in Jamaica, I wanted to stay on good terms with him. He thought I was so innocent which of course was all just an act that he gladly fell for.

Even after I left Livingston, I kept in touch with him. Just like Missouri Pimp, Joe used to tell me, "You don't have to give up the pussy, just keep making promises," and that's exactly what I did. I worked with poor Livingston, while at the same time, looking forward to being with Stocking when he got out. I even had gullible Livingston use his credit to get me an apartment and some furniture. I never let him know where I was going to put the furniture, because it was actually for Stocking and me. When the furniture came, I took it to my sister Gail's house and moved it the same day. I wanted the apartment fully furnished when Stocking got out, compliments of Livingston. I continued to lead Livingston on until the light finally came on for him; he must have gotten the message after I stopped returning his calls. I even kept the rental car until I could no longer use it. I'm sure he collected one hellacious bill, compliments of me. I can imagine that this whole thing must have been very difficult to explain to his wife; I later learned that she divorced him. While I was happy with what I got from him, I prayed I would never have to see him again by myself. Understandably, he may have been mad enough to hurt, or even kill me.

By now, Stocking had me going to Jacksonville, Florida to pick up drug money to help keep up my living. I spent most of it on Stocking's behalf, though; I was buying him a new wardrobe, among other things. While shopping, I came across this gorgeous ring. I knew it was an expensive piece but I wanted to have it appraised to be sure. A childhood friend of mine, Mary Jane, told me about her jeweler and gave me a ride over to get an appraisal. I was only going to appraise the ring, but my palm started itching once I saw all those fine pieces. What can I say? The opportunity was there. I had a big Louis Vuitton bag with me, the showcase was open, and things just started "sliding" in my bag. Mary Jane wasn't paying me any attention, but neither was anyone else, so I certainly couldn't pass up the opportunity. By the time I took the tray of diamond rings I wanted, along with my ring, I told Mary Jane I was ready to go. We left, and I was making my plans as we drove back to the Heights. She had no clue as to what had happened, until hours later. They must have contacted her to ask, but she didn't see anything, and I never told her, for fear that she might tell.

I jumped in my car and dropped off some rings for a few of my friends; I even gave Momma a nice ring. I didn't tell her it was stolen, otherwise she would never have taken it. I did use some of the rings to finance my travels, though, but the rest went to friends and family. Just as my sister always told me - I had an insatiable need to please everyone around me. To think, I was a thief without a selfish bone in my body. I often looked at thievery with a Robin Hood mindset. I never had much growing up which is what introduced me to the path I was on in the first place. I knew how it felt to go without and knew how I would've wanted someone to come through for me when I needed it. I had no problems giving or helping out my family and friends. Especially if it came from the simple task of taking from the entitled and ungrateful.

CHAPTER 13

O nce I was done with the Adapt program and all of the lessons that at the time I thought didn't apply to someone like me, I was ready to go home and get back to work. By that time, Stocking was about to get out of jail. The bad news was that he was going to be deported. I snooped around and managed to get some information from the right sources, and found out when he was leaving. I made flight arrangements and by a simple coincidence and a random chance, I ended up on the same plane, same row, and in the seat next to my man; he often wondered how I pulled that rabbit out of my hat. I stayed with him in Jamaica for a few weeks, but I had to come back. I knew he would find some way to follow me back, and sure enough, I found out the second my feet hit Miami ground that he was hopping ships. He had not been home a week and he was already back to work, beating down a whitey for a stash of weed that ended up raking in a good $100,000. We used the money to buy ourselves a brand-new BMW, cosigned by a friend who had good credit. We used the rest of the money to buy ourselves a house and abandoned the apartment that Livingston paid for.

We didn't get a chance to relax right away; my worries about Flowerman became reality the day his car drove up, and he came strolling right up to the door, he had the look of death on his face. I could tell that murder was on his mind. I instantly regretted shortchanging him, and for the first time in a very long time, I was genuinely scared. He made a beeline for me, I thought to grab my piece and had I not been in the area I was in would've shot him in an instant. Realistically, that wasn't an option for me. In just a few seconds I saw my history with Flowerman flash before my eyes. I remembered how everything went down between us, all the rumors I had heard about him, and thought of how this was about to end. My heart raced. I might as well have seen a ghost. Everything happened in slow motion but the truth of the story is that Flowerman hadn't even made it to the door before Stocking came out knowing it was a problem, ready to straighten that nut-job out. Flowerman gave my man one good look, then turned right back around and got in his car. That was the last time I ever saw him and as far as I know now, he's rotting in prison for the rest of his life, right where he belonged. Good riddance.

Once we were settled, Stocking said he wanted to see his kids in Jacksonville, so I went with him. When we got there, we came across a nasty sight: his wife had fallen victim to crack. She had a nasty addiction and was huddled up with their kids in the projects. The door was barely even hanging on the house, all the windows were busted, and everything was a filthy mess. The worst part of it all was him seeing that his kids had to live like that; we took them on the spot. They didn't even have a pair of shoes to bring with them. The next day we took them to the mall and shopped until we all dropped. Since I had better taste, Stocking let me pick out most of their items. His nine-year-old daughter, Tia, was kind of difficult at first; she was fond of her Momma and not yet very keen on me, so she did her best to play me against her father. I invented the manipulation game, and no little girl was about to beat me at it. She figured it out quickly and stopped playing. I actually started to like those kids, to the point where I didn't want to see them go back to their crack-head Momma. We decided that we would take them to Miami. With a new home and a new car, we knew life would be a whole lot better for them with us.

I kept doing hair in my spare time, and eventually, I turned the garage into a wall-to-wall carpeted beauty salon with air conditioning. I had the spot hooked up. Sure, I didn't have a permit, but like everything else in my life, I did it anyway, I had gotten away with far more malicious hustles than not having a beautician's license. Doing hair proved to me that I could indeed do anything I put my mind to. The way I saw it, at least I was trying to do a little bit of something legit. It was never much of a problem until customers started getting nosey. It probably looked suspicious to them that we were living so cozy, yet it was known that my man had no job, and I was only doing hair.

Stocking started going out sometimes without me. I didn't care as long as he spent his money on the house and on me, because I took care of everything else. I played step-mom, kept him a nice house, and even enrolled the kids in school. As soon as Tia got her new school clothes, she wanted to go back to Jacksonville. Stocking wanted none of that, but I convinced him to let her go. I knew she would soon miss her new lifestyle and want to come back. It wasn't even a week before she was ready to come back home. His little boy on the other hand, Karruh, was always an angel - completely the opposite of his sister.

The whole time I was taking care of the kids and house, I was under house arrest as an additional punishment after I was shooed out of Vegas. It was either that or more jail, and as far as I was concerned, a taste of freedom was better than nothing. It didn't stop me from wanting to beat the system, though. Since Stocking was usually away, and the kids were at school, I started getting a little stir-crazy in that house. I snuck out one day, and sure enough, when I got home my officer was waiting and took me right off to jail for violation. I was stuck in jail for four months, and in that time, everything with Stocking began to go downhill. I heard that he had some girl I didn't know driving around in my car, and from what my family told me, the house was a complete shanty. Most of the furniture was destroyed, his boys had put holes in the walls, and everything was a mess. I was beyond pissed. After all the time and effort I had put into making it a home for us, he allowed it to go down the toilet the second I wasn't there to keep it together for him.

When I was released from jail, Stocking was ashamed to face me. He knew that I would never want to be bothered with him after he had let me down. He bolted, and had the nerve to take my car with him! At first, he said it was in the shop, but I figured out his game. He thought he was slick – he reasoned, that if he kept my car I would stay around. All it really did was piss me off; especially after I found out that he painted it. I managed to get it back though, ironically, with a little help from the police. I didn't have the resources to have the house repaired, so I let it go and leased a one-bedroom apartment for myself. Fortunately, I managed to salvage some of my furniture.

I was trying to work out rebuilding my life yet again, without Stocking this time. One night, I went out with a couple of my girls to Magic City and I was drinking heavily, but by sheer chance, I ran into Stocking. While I ignored him most of the night, as I was leaving, I went over to talk to him. A chick he had been talking to earlier proceeded to interrupt our conversation. She apparently thought she had it like that with him. Pissed as I was, I was ready to put that bitch in check. But before anything really had time to jump off, Stocking had put her in the car and left. I wasn't about to take that kind of shit, so I followed them because now it seemed like Stocking tried to disrespect me. After all I had done for him, I wasn't going to happen, especially over some insignificant bitch.

I jumped out of the car once he got to her house, guns were drawn, and I was ready to fight. During the altercation, I ended up getting stabbed in the thigh. It was a good thing that all that happened because all of us were armed enough for it to have ended up a hell of a lot worse. I left for a bit, but Stocking's dumb ass had led me right to her house, and I intended to keep up the fight. I contacted a punk friend of mine called Slim, and he switched cars with me. I took his Benz and he took my BMW. I almost totaled his car while trying to run her ass over. Lucky for her, the cops showed up, and they took me to the hospital to take care of my thigh. I was there for about an hour, nixed getting stitches, and then left with revenge in mind. I was ready to settle things with that bitch.

I ended up going home that night, but the next morning, I was back at the hospital. The wound was so deep that the bleeding would not stop. She had done more damage than I realized with the butcher knife, which only pissed me off even more. I ended up having to get stitches anyway. The next day, I went looking for someone to help me get her back. A friend of mine gave me the number for this guy named Damon. I explained to him that I didn't want the bitch killed, but that I just needed her to know who in the hell she was fucking with. She clearly had no precursor or warnings about me and thought she was in the clear and won after stabbing me. Even though I called him to do the work, I still went along. After all, this was my business that he was handling. He went to work while I sat and watched from across the street. He came up to her with some story about bringing her a package. As she reached for him, he pulled out his gun and got her right in her lower body. I had someone waiting in another car for Damon. He jumped in the car, and they were gone. Within minutes, the emergency rescue was there. After they put her in the ambulance, I got in my car and followed behind. When they stopped at a red light, I wanted to stop and knock on the door and say, "Yeah bitch, who got the last laugh?" but of course I wasn't able to make it known to her who was behind her getting shot, she had no clue as to what really happened to her. Stocking, however, knew exactly what the deal was and undoubtedly knew that I came back for revenge on his harlot and got it.

I thought that ordeal would mark the end of my relationship with Stocking, so I got ready to move on. I was looking for some work and Plug Eye, the man who referred me to Damon, said he had a friend from Chicago who needed someone to go to Nassau, Bahamas; he didn't have to say anymore. I already knew what the job consisted of, and since I had experience in transporting drugs, I had no problem taking the job. The only problem was that he was only offering me 500 dollars per trip. The amount he was offering me to risk my freedom amongst other things was laughable. He must have thought I was an amateur or something. I looked at it as a test of him trying to play on my intelligence. Since I needed the money I took the job and demanded more pay. It didn't matter to me that I was in a wheelchair, with stitches holding my thigh together - I wanted my money and was going to get it by any means necessary.

After taking the job, he set me up with my new partner, a man named Gucci. After speaking with Gucci, we came up with a very fair, and reasonable, price for making the trip. He was initially quite impressed with me, but even more so when I arrived in the Bahamas in a wheelchair. The same way I went in the same way I returned, sitting on the powder, which no one even realized, was there. After all, no one was about to suspect a cripple of running drugs. When I got there he already had a couple of white chicks who worked for him in the Bahamas, but their game was pretty weak. They messed up the cocaine by crushing it into powder rather than leaving it in its original brick form. I showed them a way that they could get it by Customs, and since they were white,

Customs wasn't really going to fuck with them anyway. It was a sad, but true fact that still remains to this day.

Over in the Bahamas, the price of cocaine was $2500, but in the United States, you could retail bricks for $24,000, easily. Once I arrived, we were in business. After everything was prepared properly, we were ready to hit the road. The girls made it through Customs safely and with my wheelchair, so did I. I had my friend, Kymba along with me. She ended up being my assistant who pushed me along in the chair, which worked out well because it made the whole ruse even more convincing. Gucci couldn't believe how smoothly we pulled everything off. With my success, he began to want to see me on a personal level. He invited me up to Rochester, NY, and confessed how much he wanted to commit to me. He promised he would be all I ever needed, but I knew what he really wanted. He needed someone to compliment him and what he was doing; a bitch with beauty, brains, and bravery.

We made a stop in North Carolina, and he tried to sleep with me, but I wasn't having it. I wasn't all that convinced that he was all about me, not to mention I still had stitches in my thigh. After he tried to get up on me, I said to him flat out, "What about your woman that you have in Chicago, the one that was looking after your store? Yeah, I've done my homework, old boy." He still tried convincing me that he was willing to put all of that on hold, while he began a life with me. Really, he needed to know that I had to be number one at all times. Even after I told him that, I sensed that he still really wanted me. That was fine for me since it meant I was going to get what I wanted, regardless of the outcome.

Gucci told me to bring $50,000 to Miami for some reason, but he wouldn't tell me why. From what I gathered, he wanted me to keep the money in Miami until he gave me orders on what to do with it. I don't know if he was trying to test me or not, but it didn't matter, because

I had plans for that money the second it landed in my hands. Kymba was a little wiser than me and warned me that he was just trying to see if I would follow his orders, or go behind his back and use the money. At first, I took her advice and didn't spend the cash, but eventually, I reconsidered; I couldn't just let $50,000 sit and rot on my dresser when I knew just where it could go.

By the time Gucci came to ask me for the money, I had already given my mom and dad some of it. So, when I spoke to Gucci I came clean. Luckily, he wasn't too mad. As soon as he got back to Miami, he came to my apartment and asked how much I would need to get a brand-new bedroom set because he didn't want to sleep in the same bed that I had shared with Stocking. He proceeded to pull out a roll of money and peeled $10,000 right off the top. I smiled to myself, took the roll, and got me a new bedroom set without spending a dime. Gucci mostly knew me as a hustler and a drug runner, it might have never occurred to him that I was a jack of all street trades and got what I wanted, how I wanted to get it. I decided to keep the money and get the merchandise another way.

Me and Gucci came up quickly together. He had hookups in Rochester and Buffalo, and I had contacts in D.C. and California, which kept our circle pretty wide. Once Gucci figured out that most of my contacts were male, he was shocked. He didn't understand how I could have these types of relationships with men and not have to sleep with them. I kept telling him that it was just all in the way I carried myself. Never would I be less than a lady, regardless of what I was doing. Thank God for Momma's morals, otherwise I would have been on my back a hell of a lot more.

I went to West Hollywood, where my friend, Kelly, ran a club called Speak-Easy. He had cocaine, but his shit was garbage. I met Kelly at the Mack Ball when I was a teen, and we stayed in touch occasionally since we were good friends. Later in life, it looked like we were about to take our friendship to another level; I was about to become his supplier. Once he and I were reunited, I knew that we would work well together. Kelly knew a lot of people, and everyone loved him. He was so good that most people thought the club belonged to him, but it actually belonged to a white guy we both knew and he was just the face of it. Kelly had changed a lot since the last time I saw him. He had lost most of the characteristics of a pimp, since he had pretty much given up that lifestyle, to become a major, very conservative drug dealer. He had West Hollywood on lock. I was the only person who dealt with him because he didn't really trust anyone else. This was fine by me because, after the cast of characters and things I had been through prior, I didn't really trust anyone either.

I instantly fell in love with my new upgraded lifestyle. I had leveled up once again! Whenever I got with Gucci, all I had to do was drop off the drugs, and when he was ready I would go get the money. Gucci was impressed, and I was financially blessed. I was spending almost $10,000 a day on whatever I wanted. I would sometimes make runs through DC as well, but soon after the city started getting very dangerous and my people stopped me from making the runs. I felt pretty safe after a while, not to mention comfortable as hell with a new man, a new life, and more money than I could ever dream of or so I thought. With new levels always came new devils and it was a matter of time before they would be right at my doorstep.

CHAPTER 14

Even though he was a little softer than most of the men I rolled with, Gucci still knew how to spoil a girl. He was lavishing me with wonderful gifts: I had a brand new 300 Mercedes, midnight blue, that was paid for with cash. I still had my BMW, too. Even with all of my money and his gifts, I still missed doing what I was best at - stealing. Sometimes several of my girls and I would go out and hit a few licks. It wasn't about the money and turned into being more for the thrill. The payoff would sometimes end up not being worth the risk but the risk was worth the rush. This criminal mindset is where some can get caught up. It's like once you know it's hard to get caught it becomes even harder to stop, and when you can't stop is when you end up getting caught. Being notorious meaning also being part of a vicious cycle.

All the while, I still had groups of girls heading down to the Bahamas to pick up drugs. Sometimes, I'd go with them, too; other times I would just meet them on the island. Gucci didn't like it much at first, but I convinced him that to make money, you had to spend money. From what I could tell, we weren't really losing money, anyway. It only cost us $2500 per key, and we could sell it for ten times that, back in the States. We had enough cash to play with so, I let some of my girls take a three-day cruise. However, I only let the white girls go for one day. Some of them even started buying cars for themselves. Gucci bought himself a brand new car, a candy apple red Corvette. I was the first to drive it and

BYE BYE BLACK SHEEP

put the first 100 miles on it; I drove right in front of the club Magic City.
As I pulled up, I spotted Stocking; I hollered at him, but he did his best
to ignore me. I guessed that he wasn't really feeling what I was all about
right then, but it didn't matter anyway, so I didn't push it.

In the meantime, Stocking had settled back in Miami and was
plotting Gucci's demise. He hated the fact that I had gotten with someone
that had everything together, and knew how to run his business. Stocking
and his boys were focusing hard on plotting against Gucci. I found out
that Stocking had given orders to do anything to Gucci, but no one was
to fuck with me. I was in Memphis, and Gucci said he had just left the
house, obviously being followed. Someone was ratting, and I figured out
quickly that it was Plug Eye. He was the same one who introduced me
to Gucci, but it turned out he knew both of my men. I figured that his
loyalties must have laid more with Stocking than with Gucci. Perhaps,
he just feared Stocking more. Besides, no one ever had a real reason to be
scared of Gucci.

The men following Gucci eventually managed to get into the
house. In broad daylight, they popped the sliding glass doors, came in,
and took our safe right out of the house. There was about $60,000 in
the safe along with a half of a pound of heroin. It wasn't too big of a loss
considering that we could have both lost our lives had we been there.
As they left, they placed a pair of my stockings on the table - to let me
know who exactly had been there. As soon as I saw the stockings, I knew
Stocking had paid us a visit; he knew exactly where I laid my head and
made it known that he could get at me whenever he pleased. This made
me anxious and kept me up at night. I knew I had to move. We found a
new place quickly - a house over in the upscale Falls area.

Folks were still coming at us, mostly Gucci, though, because he
was too damn trusting. He was always getting cheated or taken for a ride

by someone. Once over in the Bahamas, we had a hook-up with a police officer named Brian. He made sure that the product made its way from Exuma to Nassau, it was going well until 25 keys came up missing. We had to straighten that out which meant with Gucci in charge we had to take a loss. For the next shipment, our prices had increased from $2500 a key to $3500. The way I saw it, if Gucci had handled his business, put his foot down, used a little bit of force, and let a few of those thugs have it they wouldn't have disrespected him like that. Instead, they played right into Stocking's hand. Stocking was bent on making Gucci's life miserable with me; at one point, one of the same thugs that screwed us before told Gucci that I was taking his money, and giving it to Stocking. Now, I don't know about Gucci, but I was definitely not stupid enough to be giving the money away that I had helped to get. Luckily, Gucci wasn't that stupid either.

I did my best to ignore Stocking and all the bullshit he was trying to pull while trying to keep up with my business at the same time. One day, I went by one of my old hustler friend's house and saw that she had an old ROTC uniform. As soon as I saw it a little light went off in my head. It looked just like a regular army uniform to me, and I could just imagine seeing Brandy sporting it. I took the uniform home and called Brandy. When she got there, I explained to her that she was being temporarily inducted into Uncle Sam's Army; she just laughed and put on the suit. The way she was acting, you would have thought she was really in the service. She even had it down to the opaque stockings; it was a perfect cover. With her uniform on and service woman act intact, would confidently take suitcases full of dope, to wherever she needed to go. Once, she was supposed to go to Nassau, but got careless and ended up taking the wrong plane – on her way to Haiti. It scared her senseless because she said that she had never seen so many guns drawn. I felt like she was overreacting at the time but in hindsight, she had over $100,000 on her body and was lucky she was able to complete the mission and make it out alive. Gucci was rightfully mad, but once she got the next plane out, I was able to calm him down. We took several risks by sending Brandy out there like that, not only was she facing being robbed or worse, but she was also impersonating the military and facing a lot of jail time had she got caught.

When the summer of 1989 rolled around, a bad hurricane tore through Jamaica. Little did I know, just over the horizon, was another natural disaster, by the name of Karma who was about to pay me a well, overdue visit. During this time, Gucci got some barrels of supplies together and went to help his family in Jamaica. I didn't care because I loved having my space. After he left, a friend of mine told me he was having a party, so I decided to go and took Kymba along with me. At this time, I was still tooting cocaine, occasionally, and this was one of the nights I decided to indulge myself. I had Kymba drive because I didn't feel comfortable knowing that I was high. The streets were so crowded, that I told her to park on the corner. I greeted some of the people I knew, and the lady of the house invited us to the back to the pool. I started to get in, but I saw this Colombian with a video camera and decided against it. Who knew what he planned on doing with the tapes or who would see them after that night, I was already paranoid but high or not, I knew I didn't want to be anywhere near that.

I went inside the house, and then into the bedroom where some personal friends were relaxing. Kymba was hanging right with me, but she didn't get high. Instead, she just chilled and had a couple of drinks. While everybody was tooting, I decided to go to the restroom. I left my purse, and when I came back, I picked up my purse and knew that I had been hit. I looked into my wallet and the few hundred dollars that I left in there was gone. I didn't trip, based on my personal history, although I never hit or stole from friends or in personal settings, I knew how folks moved. It was a swift reminder to always be wary of my surroundings. I always kept my big money on my person anyway so it wasn't all I had; still, I knew I wasn't in the right company. So I gave Kymba the eye and she knew it would be time to leave soon.

On my way out, I spotted someone I didn't want to see - Damon. He started to ask me for some drugs, but something about him was a little unsettling. I knew he was dangerous, and it didn't matter whose payroll he was on, he would certainly get the job done. By then, I was ready to leave. Kymba was already following behind and felt my vibes on making the move out the door as well, so we got ready to leave. Even though I was high, I was still alert, so I told Damon to go with Kymba to get my car from the corner. I figured I would let him keep thinking I wasn't scared, besides, it was better to keep a killer comfortable, rather than to piss him off. The whole time, I still followed my instincts. When they pulled up and he got out, I got in and told Kymba to drive. I instructed her not to go directly to the house. I had a very strange feeling that he and his boys were going to follow us. We left Perrine and ended up turning so many corners that we wound up on the beach. We eventually made it home safely, and without incident.

Just as I had suspected, the next day I found out that some guys had planned on kidnapping me. They were going to hold me for a $250,000 ransom because they knew Gucci wouldn't have a problem paying. Had I walked down to that corner, only God knows what would have happened to me. Being in the "life." you are always paranoid, that narrow escape put me more on edge than ever. It was the beginning of me not only being more careful but valuing my life and seeing things from a different perspective. Shortly after, an associate of ours, Sugar Momma, was killed. Sugar Momma was known to the chef, but she wasn't the best; she actually messed up some of our products. She claimed to know how to step on heroin, but either she was lying, or her skills had gotten rusty.

She turned our product into pure garbage; Gucci and I didn't blame her, since we were the ones who hired her. After her death, we decided to move from the Falls and relocate to Old Cutler - a cul-de-sac where the homes ranged from $500,000 up. Ironically, she knew Stocking. It was starting to feel like everyone knew him, and sometimes, it seemed like no matter where I went, or whom I spoke to, he followed me.

The detectives came to my house to question me about Sugar Momma. Someone had told them that Stocking was angry, because he went to her laundromat for a drug transaction, got cheated on the deal, and went to jail immediately after. He ended up getting out pretty quickly but because Stocking was brought up, investigators tried to connect Sugar Momma's murder to me. Although I had been serious about the game, I had never ordered a murder. It wasn't in me to do something so heinous. I prayed for God to reveal to me, who was responsible for her death. A few weeks later, I had my answer. It turned out that a man named Bobby had set up the murder, as well as the murder of another man named, Mr. Lawrence, who had been trying to clear his neighborhood of drug runners.

I remember Bobby pulled up to the car wash in Perrine to talk to me before he was arrested. When he got out, and gave them his car he said to me, "I guess you heard that they're saying that it was either you or me that had Sugar Momma killed." I had no idea, and never even heard that until he mentioned it. It turned out that Bobby had hired some young gunners from Scott Projects (Liberty City) to do the job. After the murders, one of the boys' sisters saw the news, and just knew in her heart that her brother and his boys were responsible. Bobby's cheap-ass only paid those kids $500 for the job. They sentenced Bobby to the death penalty for the conspiracy of murder. That very same night, I found out from Gucci that Sugar Momma told him I put voodoo on him; only the Lord knows why or what her motive for saying something like that was.

Supposedly, she had been the one to take me to the reading which made the story even more bizarre. Telling something like that to a Jamaican was the wrong thing and even had me shook a little considering that I've never indulged in anything like that. Still, it didn't matter what I said - Gucci was convinced.

CHAPTER 15

Even though my reign is over, my legend lives on through the memories of those who've traveled this road with me, and through the actions of those who have followed in my footsteps. My actions have affected many people, and they will continue to, for as long as people know my name.

Things were never the same after Sugga Momma died. Gucci decided to believe the things she told him and everything between us began to fall apart slowly, but surely. I found out that he was messing around with a Jamaican girl; one day he came home with new shoes and underwear. Since he never went shopping on his own, I knew someone else had bought them for him. The broad had purchased the items on her credit card, and sure enough, she left the receipt in the bottom of the bag. I knew she left it there on purpose; and was trying to make a statement. I was ready to ring her neck, but I decided to wait around. After all, I had her information now, so I was in no rush.

Two girls who worked for me, Joya and Meeka, were going with me to the islands now regularly. I worked with many girls, but these two usually tried to beat the others out, so they could go with me. They were my go-to's at that time and usually did things precisely. Still, no matter how many times we got away with it, the time comes when it's always "one time too many." I had always been particular about how the girls should dress when traveling across the water. I told them not to wear long skirts or dresses since the police looked for things like that. I always recommended short dresses, that were only full at the bottom. But of course, the day came when they weren't on top of their game, and they were being greedy. Both of them wore long dresses, and the cops got suspicious enough to check them out. It was a big mess, and they ended up getting busted with eight keys of cocaine. I was pissed, and even though I was livid at the thought of their stupidity and greed, and felt they deserved to be locked up, I couldn't ditch them like that.

Joya's brother was a Florida State Trooper, so he advised her on how she should handle the situation, while we found ways to handle it ourselves. We had already gotten them lawyers who were being paid under the table. Utilizing their services, they were guaranteed to get only one year. Joya decided that her brother, now her legal advisor, knew more than the attorneys knew, and went with his advice, which landed her ass with eight years in Nassau's prison system. For the life of me, I cannot understand how Joya and her brother thought that she would be found totally innocent after being caught red-handed with all that dope on her.

My Daddy went over to take some money for their attorneys. We still had to pay them, even though those dumb broads didn't use them. I didn't go; I was afraid that the girls might set me up, and then all of us would have been living in inhabitable conditions, locked up in a foreign, third-world-like prison. Despite their own stupidity, I was doing everything I could to keep them as comfortable as possible. Even still, they thought I snitched on them; I don't know what gave them that idea. For one, it wasn't how I rolled and furthermore, what was the logic in that? They worked for me and lost my product and my money. The only explanation I could come up with is that they probably figured that since they talked too much, and would tell on their own mommy if it meant saving their asses, I would do the same. Fortunately, I was cut from a different type of cloth.

The other girls weren't shaken by the incident, too much. As they saw it, Joya and Meeka were hogging all the trips anyway. April, who was Meeka's younger sister, started to volunteer. I decided to start setting her up with Sabrina; who was easily one of my best girls. She paid attention to instructions and details, and was always aware of her surroundings; prime ingredients that a true hustler must have. She was my ace in the hole. Despite sending her off with Sabrina, April still managed to end up on the rocks on her first ride with her. It was a close call. When they returned, I was there to pick them up. I waited for Sabrina to come out, but it took a few minutes longer than usual. I tried not to worry. Then she stepped in view, dressed properly, and wearing her four keys, but there was still no sight of April. We waited as patiently as possible, and then, twenty minutes later, she appeared, looking really nervous. She said that they searched her, but the way the dope was attached to the back of her upper thighs, she was able to pull her skirt up high enough that she didn't have to reveal anything. Thank God it was only a stewardess who searched her; had it been a regular agent, she would have gotten caught. Even though I told her to leave those long ass skirts and dresses at home, she had worn one anyway.

By now, Gucci had bought a boat. He got it for the sole purpose of sending it out to sea to collect bundles. I didn't think anything of it at first, since having the boat was a major timesaver, but right around that time, he started to become very busy, and somewhat secretive. I knew he was still sneaking around with that other girl. He wasn't even trying to hide his shady behavior now. While he thought he was a player, he ended up getting played himself. I figured out, at one point, that he was leaving money over at his girl's house, and she had taken $50,000 from him and bought herself a Toyota Cressida. He tried to hide that from me, perhaps out of embarrassment, or, perhaps, to save his own sorry ass from getting kicked, but of course, the streets talk. I really didn't care, because

I usually did the same thing she did anyway. Every time he would put some money down and didn't look at it for a while, I ended up keeping it. More than once, I went into our stash and took out thousands of dollars to tuck away for a rainy day.

Since Gucci had been so busy with the boat business, I was doing my own thing, which was keeping the house, and entertaining the kids. At this point in my life, I had a regular flock of kids who came over to the house to have a good time. I didn't mind much; actually, I quite enjoyed the company. Since I knew I could never have kids of my own, it was the closest I was ever going to get to being a mom. I used to let them come over and enjoy the pool; I even took a few out with me to the flea market, and let them pick out gifts while I had my nails done. Some of the older ones wanted to get diamonds in their nails like mine, but I had enough sense to say no to the younger ones, that was the last thing they needed to be showing off at their age.

We were still taking cruises down to the Bahamas for vacations, as well as work, so I bought 12 tickets and decided to take all of the kids on the cruise. Of course, my main objective was to meet up with an associate in Freeport, and I figured that taking the kids along wouldn't cause much of a hassle. I had never been more mistaken in my life. After that experience, I will never again take that many kids on a trip. They were all over the place. If one of them had all of a sudden decided to jump ship, I doubt I would have even noticed. Even though they had a wonderful time, my mind was a little too preoccupied to watch them as closely as I should have. It was only because of the kids that I found out one of the cruise employees was hitting on Dawn, a twelve-year-old. Of course, the employee denied everything, but my kids don't lie, and I made sure he didn't keep his job for much longer.

Now that everyone knew my game, and how deep I had gotten myself into drug running, we constantly had to be on our toes. We kept moving from Miami to Memphis, D.C., and my main spot was in California. Since I lived in Richmond Heights, which was a small town, the local police had it out for me. Every time I even thought about riding down the street, the cops were all over me. I can't count the number of times the police stopped me for the most bogus reasons. One evening, they stopped me and claimed I had switched drivers. Truthfully, all they wanted to do was harass me. Even with all of the nonsense they tried to pull with me, eventually, they did manage to pull me over and get a legitimate reason to take me in. Out of sheer dumb luck, they stopped me near my sister's house on a supposed "routine check." What they found out was that my license had been suspended, which was news to me. I knew I was going to be arrested, but I wasn't so worried about that. I was more worried that they would find the .38 caliber revolver stashed in the car. Once I figured out that they were going to take me to the station, I quickly hid the gun on my body, since I figured that they were going to search my car. Thankfully, since I was so close to my sister's house, I had someone call her, and tell her to come to the site and pick my car up, so it wouldn't be towed. As they were taking me to the police station, all I could think about was whether I should have left the pistol in the car. However, since I figured I would make a bond the second I stepped foot in jail, I stood a better chance of disposing of it myself.

They placed me in a holding cell, where I listened in on the cops. I wasn't worried; I knew, that no matter how much the bond was set for; somebody would pay for it, in cash. My father had gotten the money from Gucci and came down to bail me out, so they let me out of the cell to wait while the paperwork was being done. I was home free, but for some strange reason, the officer decided that she needed to strip-search me. I thought, "Damn, if I had known that, I would have left the gun in the cell." It was too late to go back, and I couldn't think of a good excuse to go back into my cell without making the cops suspicious. When the female officer came up to me, I was literally sweating bullets.

I knew there was no way I was going to talk my way out of the situation. There was no place for me to get rid of the pistol, so I kept my mouth shut and waited for the inevitable. The officer who found the gun almost had a heart attack. The bullets were still in the chamber, and the way she reacted, you would have thought there was a terrorist attack or something. Since she had to leave her gun at a checkpoint, I was the only one that was armed. I'd never seen a cop so flustered in all of my life - the girl was so freaked out, that it was almost pathetic. I told her, "Bitch, please, ain't nobody trying to do nothing to you, so stop exaggerating the situation." I was flustered by the situation as well, shit, I was the one who was caught and going to catch charges from it, not her. This showed me one thing I knew to be true about the police though, and that was that they weren't shit without a badge and even less than shit without a gun. I wasn't thinking about shooting her but the fear in her heart and on her face proved that she was hiding behind her blue shield like the rest of them.

What started out as a minor traffic violation, escalated to a full-blown gun charge. Nevertheless, I still managed to make a bond. Even though I was out for the time being, I knew my freedom was going to be short-lived. Being a convicted felon with a gun was automatically a sentence for three years, or more. I had to prepare, for what I knew was the inevitable, which was being on lock for a minute. If that wasn't enough trouble, I was still running into all sorts of drama outside of jail.

One day, while over at my Mom's house, I found out that Gucci had run out to see another girl. It was the same whore who had bought him those clothes. What was even more insulting, he had the nerve to ride over to her place in my car. I was pissed, and I was ready to get even. I had always kept that address in the back of my mind; I figured the information would come in handy someday and today was the day. The address wasn't far from where my mother lived, so I jumped in his car and drove on over. True enough, my car was parked in front of this bitch's house. I blew the horn repeatedly, waited for him to come out, and then peeled off. I'm sure the first thought that flew through his mind was that I was going to take all of his money and run off somewhere. He immediately came to my mother's house, driving so fast that he even tore across her lawn. When he jumped out of that car and started banging on my Momma's door, he had the nerve to act like I was the one in the wrong. I said, "Child please, you were caught with your hand in the cookie jar, not me." He tried to intimidate me, and demanded I give his keys back, but I was going to do no such thing. He had picked a bad day to try to mess with me. Daddy was home, and seeing Gucci trying to act all bad had set his teeth on edge. All my Daddy knew was that Gucci was disrespecting his home, his daughter, and his wife.

Before I could even think about stopping him, Daddy was trying to take Gucci out. At first, I was happy helping out Daddy. Gucci wanted his keys, but all he ended up getting from me was a telephone upside his head. Eventually, things got so heated that Daddy went to get his gun. By then, the commotion had the neighbors on alert, and they were coming outside to see what was happening. Momma was hysterical, begging Daddy to get off of Gucci, even though I wasn't too worried about Daddy killing him. He just wanted to put him in his place. The whole time he was knocking him senseless, he told him never to come to his house, and disrespect him, or his wife again. Daddy finally let him go, and I threw him his keys as he went running off. I decided not to go home that day, not that I was scared -I was just too furious to trust myself. As always, Gucci was too much of a softie for me to really be afraid of him.

CHAPTER 16

Karma was sitting in my living room, and it refused to leave. I had gotten a charge, Meeka and Joya had been busted in the Bahamas, and Gucci was still getting robbed from time to time. Trina, my Goddaughter, had even gotten busted in Memphis when she went to do a drop-off. Gucci and Daddy still weren't speaking, but for some odd, yet wonderful,reason, Daddy and I had gotten really close. For the first time, I was proud to be my Daddy's daughter, and happy to say that I was just like him. He was tied to a lot of unpleasant memories from my younger years but life had taken a full circle and showed me how life had made him the way he was and also how we both came out better because of it.

Memorial Day weekend rolled around, and one of the girls, Portia, wanted to make a trip. It was risky because she was a couple of months pregnant, but that didn't deter either of us. We were still collecting keys from Nassau; air traffic was tight, and the warning signs in my head were flashing bright red. I should have listened and taken heed to the signals my body was telling me, my instincts were rarely wrong. Despite my hesitation, I stuck to the plan; I was going to fly over there and let her come down the next day, but I was running late leaving the house. By the time we had arrived at Miami International, and I got to the counter, I didn't have a passport or birth certificate. Thankfully, the reservationists still let me fly but informed me that I would need the documents for re-entry. I didn't care, because I was on a mission that I was not about to abort. I had to get my sister Gail to fly over, and bring me the documents. I told Gail to catch the early flight back, and I would follow on a later flight. She kept on insisting that she take the drugs instead of me, but I was having none of that. I kept waiting for Portia to come, but she never showed. I knew I was running out of options. Gucci never wanted me to ever touch or carry drugs as of late, but this once I thought it would be alright. God had given me 100 warning signs, but my hard head wasn't looking or listening.

The moment I got to Miami, and had one foot out of the door, the paranoia set in. Even though I looked innocent, I felt like all eyes were on me. My mind lingered on the possibility that I was being set up. On top of everything, I had just fired this punk from my crew for gossiping about my organization, and he had promised me that he was going to tell all the muggers and all of the alphabet boys (DEA, FBI, ATF, IRS, etc.) about me and my business. I thought it was a bluff, but in that overcrowded airport with a million eyes on me, I was starting to have second thoughts.

Well, thanks to that punk, and my ever-lingering friend, karma, I got busted. I went to jail, on May 31, 1989. I was charged with transporting four keys of cocaine. As I was waiting to make bond, I had to go to the Magistrate who informed me that he was issuing a bond with Nebbia, which was a stipulation that mandated I divulge where every last dime of my bond money was coming from. Based on the circumstances, that took some extra time. On June 5th, I was in jail, speaking to my Dad on the phone about the bond, and he took responsibility for speaking to the bondsman. He was supposed to meet him at around 4:00 pm. I had spoken to Daddy several times that same day, but I couldn't fathom or make up the next series of events. I had no idea what was about to unfold.

My sister, Gail, was home with Daddy, along with her six-year-old daughter, Tiffany, and Brandy's daughter, Dawn. Momma was still at work driving the school bus. Daddy had already spoken to the bondsman, and Gucci had given Daddy the money. Gail said that Daddy left, but came back in very quickly; she thought he had forgotten something. He sat on the side of the bed but didn't say anything. She was in the next room, about five feet away from him, but didn't say anything to him before she headed into the kitchen. My niece, Tiffany, went into the bedroom to say something to Daddy and noticed his eyes were rolled back into his head. Terrified, she ran to her mother and told her something was terribly wrong with her grandfather. Gail went to check on him, and he wasn't breathing. In just a matter of a few minutes, my Daddy fell victim to a fatal heart attack. He must have felt something was about to happen for him to come back into the house that quickly.

I was already panicking before I knew about my father's heart attack; I wanted to find out what was going on with the bondsman. I kept calling the house, but no one picked up. I called repeatedly for several hours before I finally found out what happened. An officer came to my cell and asked me to come out. I was already worried, and when she took me to the staff phone, it only got worse. When I picked up the phone and heard my mother's trembling voice, I couldn't imagine what she was about to say. She asked me if I was sitting or standing, and then quietly told me that Daddy was dead. For a second, I didn't know how to breathe. I couldn't think, I couldn't move; it was a wonder that I was still standing. In all but a few minutes, my world had come crashing down. I dropped the phone and screamed. I was distraught; my father was dead, and what was worse, he had died while on his way to help me. For all the grief I put him through, he still tried to help me. For a while I just sat there crying, unsure of what to do with myself. I still had to go to court the next day, but now, Daddy wouldn't be there to help me.

When the Magistrate went back to review the questions that my Dad had answered on the bond paperwork, there were some discrepancies. She mentioned that he indicated I had never been arrested, even though he knew I had; he couldn't have understood the question. She continued down the list without even a single condolence for my loss. I hadn't a clue how someone could ever be so cold. Nevertheless, by the grace of God, she approved the bond, but it came with a long list of stipulations. So many that I was afraid the bondsman was going to reconsider. She even went so far as to say that if I so much as put one toe out of line once I was out, she was going to strip him of everything he ever had. Parham, the bondsman, told me the only reason he was going ahead and completing the process was because he knew my father died while trying to get me out. He knew I would not run; and besides, I needed to be home with my family and attend my father's funeral. I was just glad to be out and relieved that he had a heart.

A lot was on my plate; a gun charge, drug charges, and now I had to plan a funeral. Gucci took the loss almost as hard as I did. He and Daddy had just started talking again since the fight. This was great because I was in no emotional position to be concerned about Gucci. We had a service for Daddy, but he left instructions that he wanted to be cremated. Momma said Daddy always said that he did not want any bugs crawling on him, which is why he didn't want to be buried. After the service, I went home, but my sisters went with the casket to get Daddy cremated. I went into the house to sit by Gucci, who all of a sudden and out of the blue started screaming like a lunatic. Alarmed, I asked him what was wrong, and he hysterically said that he felt Daddy sitting on him. I didn't have time for his nonsense, so I just glowered at him and said, "Good, now you know he's still looking after me." Right after the funeral, I didn't have any time to relax. During the summer, I had to get busy, because I didn't know how much time I had left on the street. One thing was for certain, though, I was on my way to prison. I had hired a high-profile attorney, but the only thing he could do for me really was to keep my case from being acquitted. All I really could do was buy myself time, so I kept as busy as I could. Right before Daddy died, and while I was still in jail, Gucci was robbed. We lost almost everything: a good $200,000, the car, even the boat got jacked - I had a lot of rebuilding to do. I was stacking up on all the "credit" I could get. I was in every business imaginable. Sometimes fate would reward me, even when I didn't want to hit. I made myself available to every "Open House" possible on the weekends. I spent my weekdays at all sorts of different stores: travel agencies, phone stores, and especially hospitals. Nurses and doctors always had the best credit. I had so much "credit" that when I approached a certain jeweler downtown, he would let me purchase all types of pieces, worth between five and fifteen thousand dollars. Whatever the credit card would take, I could get. At one point, he would let me come, run the credit card myself, and get the authorization code.

Sabrina and I were near Palm Beach and stole a purse that had ID, a checkbook, credit cards, and the account code information. I went straight to the bank and withdrew $5,000.00. I had to keep the window partially up because the license was that of a white female. If the teller got suspicious, I was pretending to be the woman's driver, which would be plausible in that area of town. However, I never made anyone leery and folks would trust me very easily. After we left the bank, I spotted a jewelry store that we went to immediately. I knew what to say in "rich folk" talk, which gained their trust. Since I had trained Sabrina, she was able to collaborate on everything that I was saying. Sabrina would pretend to be my daughter and would dress the part. Since she had a mouth full of gold teeth, I would not let her do a lot of talking. I had gold teeth also, but knew how to keep them from showing. As we were casing the jewelry store, I distracted the salesperson while Sabrina cased for the safe. Lo and behold, she found it and as I hoped, it was wide open. I continued to talk to the salesperson while Sabrina removed every Rolex in the case. Sometimes, she would say, "Momma, I need to use the bathroom," and I would reply, "Honey, you have to wait until we leave, because there isn't a public facility in here." From there, we always had them; the clerk, feeling bad, would always apologize, and say that she could use their restroom. All I had to do was keep them distracted while Sabrina went into the back, and snooped around for loose cash and credit cards. With Sabrina's help, I kept on stacking.

Everybody thought I was crazy because I kept talking about how I was going to prison while still committing crimes. All I was doing was making sure I would be all right going in; I just had to be a little more careful than I usually was. I knew that if I slipped up, I would go to jail as one broke bitch - and that was *not* about to happen.

Gucci and I were still having problems, especially after all that nonsense with that girl, and him getting robbed. I met up with an associate of his, named Zoom, who only stood 5'1 which made me look like a stallion. At first, it was about business, but since he was attracted to me, I decided to play it by ear and see if we could maybe take it to a more personal level. After all, it never hurt to have another intimate connection, especially if I could take advantage of him. He and I began discussing our prices, and we came up with an excellent agreement. There was a catch though; I had to put time and money into going and picking up the product. By now, I knew that it wasn't a safe, or smart, idea for me to go, so I hired a white girl to make the trip for me. Quite naturally, she didn't have a problem with putting in the work. Being white, she had zero chance of getting busted.

I didn't let Gucci find out, but I had to eventually sleep with Zoom. It was the only time I put my good morals aside and went to bed with a man for the sake of business. I can honestly say it was the worst sex I ever had. He told me he had several kids but I was wondering where they came from, because, let's just say, he wasn't "equipped" for the job. I just laid back, watched the football game, and let him enjoy his ride. Things were closing in on me so of course I was moving in ways I hadn't before, yet still sticking to my personal morals and the code of the streets. I was enjoying my freedom and setting myself up to make sure I would be ok when I went in.Although I never wanted to sleep with Zoom, it was necessary in the grand scheme of things. There was no harm on either of our part and the only foul was that he was terrible in bed. The clock was ticking and every little thing I could do to make things more comfortable for me was necessary.

CHAPTER 17

By the summer of 1989, my world began crashing down around me. Everything that could have gone wrong, did, including being robbed again. Gucci was out of town in New York trying to get some money back. I was just returning from one of my most profitable runs, so my mood had been considerably cheery. However, all of that drastically changed once I came home to discover that someone had broken into our half-million-dollar home with all of our TVs and jewelry missing. We did not have any removable safes in the house, so they hadn't managed to get the big money. While I was taking inventory of everything that had been stolen, I quickly noticed that Daddy's ashes were missing. At first, I thought Gucci had just moved them again. He was so afraid of them and had tried moving them into the garage before, thinking they might have put some kind of voodoo on the house. When I checked the garage, they were not there, and my heart began to tighten. I ran through that house half a dozen times and turned over everything that could have been moved before my worst fears were realized. Those idiot thieves had taken my father's ashes probably thinking it was drugs. I barely had time to mourn my most recent loss when I received a second phone call from an associate of mine, I immediately realized that they were distraught. While Gucci was in New York, he was caught laundering money and landed himself in prison. Because he wasn't a citizen, the police refused to grant him a bond. Since he had been found with drugs on him during the raid, the police sent him right back to Jamaica, leaving me to handle our business without his aid. So here I was, not only dealing with facing prison time of my own but a break-in, still mourning my father's death (and his stolen ashes), and now left with a drug business owned by a man who had been deported.

I tried to shake it off and rebuild by returning to my regular habits, but the cops were a bit more clever than I gave them credit for. My jeweler whom I was using at the time told me that the cops had been by his store to question him because many of the credit cards that had been stolen were being used there. Irritably, he mentioned that his credit authorization had been temporarily revoked until the investigation had ceased. More for my benefit than his, I avoided that spot for a while.

My bittersweet end was fast approaching. I had been having a pretty good day and had gone out for some legitimate shopping. I went over to one of my favorite stores, Bloomingdale, to pick up my favorite cologne, because I was running a little low. Evidently, they were more aware of my behavior pattern than I thought. I went into another store, purchased some exotic fish for the tank, and decided to head on over to pick up the cologne. I had already been there several times and had used stolen credit, but since the cards were still working, I figured it would be cool. I pulled up in front of the store and left Kymba, who was with me, to wait in the car while I went in. It was my intention, to be in there for only half a second. As soon as I had completed the transaction, and had made it halfway to the car, the police swarmed in on me. I didn't even have a chance to explain myself. Moreover, it wasn't like there was much I could say; considering I had some of the stolen credit cards on me.

Once I received my charges, I knew it would be just a matter of time before everything started to catch up to me. I had a federal gun charge because I was a convicted felon, a drug trafficking charge for the importation of cocaine, and credit card fraud, and they even tried to convict me of burglary. Thankfully, I still had the opportunity to make a bond. After getting out yet again, I knew that I had better get all the money I could while I was still able to. I thought if I could grind and get at least $100,000, that would be enough to hold me down for a minute. I was trying to beat the clock because once I was given a court date, the police were going to know that I had too much going on.

It was like I had watched my entire existence happen all at once in a matter of months. I had reached the top of the drug game, won, lost, succeeded, failed, and still, the way I made a name for myself was by doing what I had always done, stealing. The papers referred to me as, "The Finger Nail Bandit." Since they didn't know my real name. They reported that I was prowling businesses in South Florida, taking undetermined amounts of cash and credit cards. The police even knew I spoke Potwah (patois), a type of broken English. Even though they didn't have a full description, I knew it would only be a matter of time before someone would recognize me. After all, I had been through, all the things I had gotten away with, and the massive come-ups I had made I was in a numb state thinking that it was about to end.

I should have known better than to get comfortable because, for whatever reason, my bond was revoked. The next thing I knew, I had the police hounding me all over again. I was at my parents house when I heard the sirens. When I looked outside, I saw that they had surrounded our neighbor, Mrs. Mary's house. Mrs. Mary knew that I was next door because she could see my car parked on the side of the house. Fortunately, the police did not recognize my car or the fact that they were at the wrong house. Mrs. Mary could have said, "You fools are at the wrong house!", and pointed them in the right direction, but she didn't. Mrs. Mary had been protecting my hide since I was a kid, and she was doing it all over again. With her help, I had bought an extra couple of days of freedom, which I desperately needed. In the meantime, I tried to secure my house for when I went to prison, but I couldn't find anyone who could afford it. I didn't want to put any money into it, since there was the off chance I might not have been able to keep it once I went away. Since the house was in my sister's name, I prayed that she would take care of it in case something bad went down.

I hopped from place to place, avoiding the cops for as long as I could, before finally I knew my time was up, and I surrendered. I patiently sat in jail awaiting the outcome of my charges. On the date of my ill fate, I received twenty-eight months for the federal gun charge, then one hundred twenty-one months for the cocaine charge running consecutively. The credit card and fraud state charges were run concurrently with the federal charges.

It didn't really matter to me that I was in prison -I intended to keep as cozy as possible. Of course, I took advantage of the situation; they left me no choice. With my charm, smarts, and way with people, I was able to create a system for myself that worked in my favor. It wasn't my fault some of the officers wanted what I had. I would have been an idiot not to take advantage of that. I was doing some of their hair; two of them had even borrowed some of my clothes. I was able to eat well every day, just as I would have if I were on the streets. I even had people dropping food off at the window for staff, while in actuality it was for me. The captain of the jail wasn't as easy to persuade, though. She accused me of manipulating her officers and promptly called the state to pick me up. I had things going perfectly, and now this bitch was trying to throw a monkey wrench in the works. After they came to pick me up, I figured they couldn't do that, so I called my attorney, and after around thirty days, they had to bring me back. Then I found out, that because of some ridiculous clause, the state overrode my attorney. They had it out for me but I still kept fighting for my freedom as well as my comfort while in prison.

I ended up being sent to what was considered the big house, Lexington, Kentucky to serve my ten-year bid. I couldn't have been luckier under the circumstances. During the time, of 1990, Lexington was a complete joke. We wore our own clothes, kept our jewelry, and even were allowed to wear weave. Better yet, the entire facility was coed. Nevertheless, after the first few months of rotting in that pit, I didn't have any interest in the men.

Still, no matter how lax the rules were, it was a prison and I wouldn't wish to have your freedom revoked on my worst enemy. This country was built on enslaving us as a people and the prison system was just an extension of that. Although I had certainly done the crimes, I still believe that it didn't warrant the time I did. Unless you were a rapist or murderer, there was no justifying the time most people behind bars do. Drugs, Credit Cards, Jewels, and the things I took were property that can and was replaced just as fast as it was taken. Meanwhile, the years, memories, and opportunities to start over, try again, and build a better life were taken and stretched out for as long as the government decided it wanted it to. There were people I was incarcerated with who were doing double-digit numbers for petty quantities of drugs and minor infractions. People who had their whole lives taken away for minor mistakes. Being in prison was something that undeniably changed people, it was simply up to the person if it changed you for the greater good or if it institutionalized you and made you worse than when you went in. Thankfully for me, I was able to see the silver lining in being locked up, and in turn just like everything else in my life, turn it into gold.

CHAPTER 18

After nearly ten years, I completed my sentence in 1998. I came out unprepared for how much things had changed. It was as if time had moved forward in the rest of the world, while I had been left behind. However, I was extremely grateful for the love I received upon returning home. Hurricane Andrew had destroyed the south of Miami so not only did I come home to a new environment as far as how things looked, some family members had moved. My sister Gail to Atlanta along with my favorite cousin, Jeff and my aunt had moved to Orlando. One pleasant change that I came home to was my nephew, Nate Webster, who was just a young kid when I went in and was now at the University of Miami. I began to know some of his teammates which included some of the most respected NFL players to this day. I had the pleasure of spending time with many of them including; Edgerin James, Bubba Franks, Ed Reed, Santana Moss, Reggie Wayne, Andre Johnson, Rod Mack, Damon Lewis, and Al Blades, who was later killed. Other football greats such as Najeh Davenport, Bryant McKinney, and Jeremy Shockey would often come over to my house twice a week and enjoy a special home-cooked meal. As Ed Reed would say, "It was a privilege for them to come over" As usual, I enjoyed spending time and playing an integral role in the lives of young people since I have no children of my own. Because of these relationships, I eventually ended up in a space where I was coming face to face once again with "Sharks", although different from the ones

I encountered on the streets, now I was swimming with some of the toughest guys in business out there like Drew Rosenhaus, a football sports agent and his brother Jason.

None of these friends and associates of my nephew ever judged me. They were wonderful young men, and I felt honored that they wanted to hang out with Nate at my home. My doors were always open to them. I never had a motive for surrounding myself with football players, it just happened because of my nephew's friendship with them. As I opened my house to the players, Drew Rosenhaus pretended to befriend me and would manage to get himself invited to my house depending on what football players were coming over. He was particularly interested in the players that were highly profiled for upcoming drafts. He had become a permanent fixture around my house when the boys were over, even though he was limited to what he was able to discuss with any of them because of NCAA policy. Well okay, I went for his "game," and he used me to serve his purpose. In hindsight, the way my home and my gatherings were used wasn't a good feeling for me. The Miami Hurricanes' football team had just won a trip to the Rose Bowl and it was the same time that I had violated my probation while trying to get my life in order. I was still running into snakes and sharks. The old me would have taken what I could and manipulated them as they were seemingly doing to me. However, it turned out to be a humbling experience and a lifelong lesson because I was not about to give up on my old ways.

Eventually, Drew found out that I had to go back to prison and I wasn't thrilled about him knowing because I was not ready or open about people knowing my past. However, now as I see life on the outside, I am much more open to it. It is important that people know who I was and how it plays a role in who I am while I continue to have to face the snakes and the sharks who may try to hold my past against me.

Later, I ended up befriending Najeh's mom, Carolyn, the first positive person and true friend that I've known. It was obvious to me that things had changed in the world and within myself. After being gone so long, I felt as if change was something I needed to move forward in my life. I practically grew up behind bars. I had spent nearly my whole life dodging bullets and stealing money. All I was used to were con artists, drug dealers, pimps, hoes, and thieves. I was a stranger even to my own family. My sisters grew up without me by their side, other than to ask for money or wrangle them into my dealings there was no real connection there. By now, my sisters were grown, with sons and daughters who knew me only as their eccentric aunt who occasionally stopped by to drop off a gift or two.

What hit me the hardest was when I saw what was becoming of my niece, Celeste. Already she was trying to live up to her namesake, and gradually began slipping further and further into a world I was fighting to get out of. I remembered then what my cousin had told me on the day of her birth. He told me, "Celeste, they sure fucked up when they named that baby after you." I didn't want to see her end up like me, just for the sake of living up to my so-called "legacy." To prevent that, I needed a new life. All I had to do was obtain the courage to want something different.

I decided to take my show on the road in a different way. As my cousin, Jeff used to tell me, "Cousin, you are an entrepreneur." I decided to take his advice. With his support, I found I had the capability of putting my sharp tongue to better use. But, I also found that as I grew as a person, my view of others was slowly beginning to change. For so long I had a single perspective etched into my mind, one shaped by discrimination. Where before I couldn't so much as look at a white man without wanting to spit on him, I now find myself laughing along with my nieces and nephews as they hang out with their white friends.

The changes I made cannot all be accredited to my own perseverance. Without the help of my family, and a few special friends, I would still be spiraling downwards. My family no matter the distance has always been my light in the darkness. Whenever I felt weak and likely to go astray, family members like Jeff were there to support me and set me straight once again. My friend, Carolyn, became my rock, and just about the only legitimately clean friend I have ever had in my whole life. She believed in me when I did not believe in myself and taught me the true meaning of love and trust. But my greatest inspiration has always been my nieces and nephews, and my God-children each of which I love dearly. I may never have the opportunity to have children of my own, but whenever I am in the presence of the children that have come up for me I feel as if God is giving me a chance to know the love a mother feels.

I felt compelled to share my story because I know that so many others are where I was. Today, you see many old pimps such as Don Juan being glorified. He is always on the set with Snoop Dog and other celebrities. A lot of them have already been to jail themselves. But being a celebrity does not discriminate against you from the possibility of going to prison. During my years in prison in Lexington, I served time with billionaire Leona Helmsley. It certainly made me realize how easily life can change and how titles, things, fame, and riches are just surface distractions that could never replace peace, joy, and freedom.

My sister used to tell me all the time, I had a "disease to please." She might have been right then, but today, her words have taken a completely new meaning to me. I do not wish to please but to teach others just how easy it is to lose sight. Even now, I have had to stay strong, remain focused, and mold myself into a legitimate businessperson. Avoiding the company of my past has helped me move positively toward the future. I will never know how the end will turn out, but whatever lies ahead for me, I am ready. No matter how hard the road, I have become stronger.

No longer do I need to look for the rush I used to crave? No longer am I a person that needs to please. Anyone and everyone I encounter will be given the choice to either accept me for me, both good and bad, or keep on moving.

At one time, I may have been one of the most notorious and feared females to step into the game. However, the queen of crime and mistress of manipulation has certainly stepped down from her throne. I am not afraid, nor will I miss my crown. This time by the grace of God, his goodness, and his mercy, I will rise to even greater heights.

Although entertaining, this story was not written to just document my life and the criminal climate from the 60s to the 90's. It was also written to show how accumulating money and property is fickle and not at all worth what's on the other side of the coin. This story is a precautionary tale. Everything I mentioned and have engaged in still exists just on a more progressive and modern level. Petty thievery, jewel heists, high-level credit card scams, pimping, robbery, and drug trafficking have not slowed down one bit. In fact, these crimes are more advanced and more intricate than one who lived in the early days of it could have imagined.

Yet, what also still exists is systemic racism, the prison system, stick-up men who rob and murder the top players, and the threat of losing your life and freedom at any given moment for being a willing participant in a life of crime. I am here to testify and to tell you that none of it is worth wiping out your entire existence or in the best case wiping out a large portion of your years that could be spent enjoying what freedom has to offer. If you are stuck in the struggle and have the courage and foresight to change, don't question whether you should leave the game or not. Question whether you are ready for the game to take you out first and you will always find your answer. Outsmart the game and save yourself.

EPILOGUE

Just like taking your first toot, hit or sip, fast money can make you an addict, so can conning, flim flamming, swindling and thievery. Most people don't address these issues as such, but once something controls and consumes your total existence, you are an addict who is no different from those who have other vices. I denied the fact for years that I was a kleptomaniac. Then, one night I ran into the store to pick up a few cosmetics. Even though I had close to $60,000.00 in my purse, compulsively, I had to slide something into my pocket. Unfortunately, the items had buzzers on them and when I went through the detector, it went off. That night lady luck was on my side. I ended up convincing them to allow me to pay for the items and was able to leave with only a little humiliation, rather than stacking on another charge.

The real healing started when I dropped the mask and got honest with myself. I was tired, tired of running, tired of pretending, tired of surviving instead of just living. So turned inward. I prayed, I listened, I surrounded myself with voices that poured into me instead of draining me. I wanted more for myself and I started to believe I deserved more.

That doesn't mean the temptation doesn't disappear overnight. The same hustle mentality I had then fuels my ideas, my creativity, and my entrepreneurship even now in my 70's. You don't have to change or limit who you are or who you've always been, just change the direction you are moving in. There is power in reinvention and there's peace in choosing yourself.

Take it from a OG Trap Queen, an American Gangster herself who's lived through decades of some of the best and worst, richest and poorest of times; it always gets better and what's next always outdoes what happened. Your story isn't over and neither is mine.

ABOUT AUTHOR

Celeste Wells was born in Miami Beach, Florida, and raised in the close-knit community of Richmond Heights during the final years of segregation. As the daughter of hardworking parents, she witnessed the stark realities of economic inequality from an early age—an experience that fueled her ambition and resilience. At seventeen, Celeste had her first encounter with the justice system, marking the beginning of a complicated chapter that would earn her the infamous nickname "The Fingernail Bandit." Known for her boldness, style, and street smarts, she became a symbol of both notoriety and survival.

In 2025, Celeste shared her story of transformation on *BET's American Gangster: Trap Queens*, recounting her rise, fall, and powerful redemption. Today, she is a passionate social justice advocate, the inventor of the patented **Save My Edges**™ wig band, and the proud owner of **Auntie's Key to Life Juice Bar**.

Celeste now lives in Broward County, Florida, where she continues to empower others through her advocacy, entrepreneurship, and hard-won wisdom.

ACKNOWLEDGEMENTS

from Celeste Wells

I dedicate this book to my angels above. To my mother and father, Iris and Chester Wells—your love, strength, and lessons shaped every part of me. Though you're no longer here, your spirit guides me daily. Thank you for teaching me to rise with grace, love without limits, and hold on to faith even in the dark.

To my sister Gailyn Wells, I miss you dearly. And to Debra Baum, known to many as Brandy, you live on in my heart. I know you're both whispering to God, pushing Him to walk with me. Your spirits give me courage, and your memory gives me strength. I will always love you.

I love you, my sisters by blood. To every sister I've gained through our time behind prison walls, thank you. We were forged in fire and emerged unbreakable. Your strength, loyalty, and love supported me when I couldn't stand alone. You are part of my story, my survival, and my soul.

And to all my family and friends—you know who you are. Your love, support, and belief in me kept me going. *Bye Bye Blacksheep* isn't just my story—it's a tribute to everyone who stood by me. Thank you for walking this journey with me.

www.ingramcontent.com/pod-product-compliance
Lightning Source LLC
Chambersburg PA
CBHW052134270326
41930CB00012B/2887